A Content-Based Writing Book

mosaic one

This is an 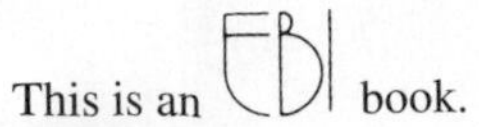 book.

McGraw-Hill 

A Division of The **McGraw-Hill** *Companies*

Mosaic One
A Content-Based Writing Book
Third Edition

4 5 6 7 8 9 0 DOC DOC 9 0 9 8

ISBN 0-07-005849-0
ISBN 0-07-114509-5

This book was set in Times Roman by Monotype Composition Company, Inc.

The editors were Tim Stookesberry, Bill Preston, and Eden Temko; the designers were Lorna Lo, Suzanne Montazer, Francis Owens, and Elizabeth Williamson; the production supervisor was Patricia Myers; the cover was designed by Francis Owens; the cover illustrator was Celia Johnson; the photo researcher was Cindy Robinson, Seaside Publishing; illustrations were done by David Bohn and Lori Heckelman.

R. R. Donnelley & Sons Company, Crawfordsville, IN, was printer and binder.
Phoenix Color Corporation was cover separator and printer.

Library of Congress Catalog Card Number: 95-80833

INTERNATIONAL EDITION

When ordering this title, use ISBN 0-07-114509-5

Literary acknowledgments and photo credits

Literary acknowledgments: *Pages 30–32* "Where Colleges Fail Us" from *The Case Against College* by Caroline Bird; *76–77* "Cynicism and Mistrust Tied to Early Death" by Sandra Blakeslee, Jan. 17, 1989. Copyright © 1989 by The New York Times Company. Reprinted with permission; *94–95* "Small World" adapted and abridged from *American West Airlines Magazine*, March 1994; *114–115* "Valley Visionaries: A World of Talent," by Tom Abate, *San Francisco Examiner*, Oct. 3, 1993; *153–154* "Defining Creativity for Everyone to See Wasn't Exactly Easy" by Bill Moyers, *Smithsonian*, vol. 12, no. 10, Apr. 19, 1978; *173–174* "Nonverbal Behavior: Some Intricate and Diverse Dimensions in Intercultural Communication" by Fathi Yousef, Ph.D. from *Intercultural Communications: A Reader*, second edition, by Larry A. Samovar and Richard E. Porter. © 1976 by Wadsworth Publishing Company, Inc. Reprinted by permis-sion of Wadsworth Publishing Company, Belmont, California 94002 and Fathi Yousef; *197–198* "Raising Cain on Values" by William J. Bennett, *Newsweek*, Apr. 18, 1994, p. 23; *p. 211* "Time to an Styrofoam?" Adapted from Paul Raiber, *Coop News*, Sept. 30, 1987; *pp. 223–224* Adapted by per-ission of the author and publishers from *Never in Anger: Portrait of an Eskimo Family* by Jean L. iggs, Cambridge, MA: Harvard University Press, Copyright © 1970 by the President and Fellows of rvard College; *240–242* "The Lowest Animal" by Mark Twain, *The Accommodating Reader*, Graw-Hill, 1992.

book is printed on acid-free paper.

A Content-Based Writing Book

Laurie Blass

Meredith Pike-Baky
University of California, Berkeley

The McGraw-Hill Companies, Inc.

New York St. Louis San Francisco Auckland Bogotá Cara
London Madrid Mexico City Milan Montreal New Delhi
Singapore Sydney Tokyo Toronto

Photo credits: *Page 1* © Michael Newman/PhotoEdit; *2 (top)* © John Fung; *(bottom)* © Walter Gilardetti; *3 (top)* © Gale Zucker/Stock, Boston; *(middle top)* © Suzanne Arms/The Image Works; *(middle bottom)* © Walter Gilardetti; *(bottom)* © Dan Chidester/The Image Works; *6* © Peter Menzel/Stock, Boston; *21 (left)* © Tom Wagner/SABA; *(right)* © Figaro Magann/Photo Researchers, Inc.; *25* © Frank Tapia; *26 (left)* © Walter Gilardetti, Courtesy of Computer Learning Center, Somerville, MA; *(top right)* © Seth Resnick/Stock, Boston; *(bottom right)* © Richard Pasley/Stock, Boston; *29* © Elizabeth Crews/Stock, Boston; *32* © M. Antman/The Image Works; *41* © Chris Andrews; *42* © Bob Daemmrich/Stock, Boston; *47* © Stuart Cohen; *49* © Tony Freeman/PhotoEdit; *50 (left)* © Francis Owens; *(right)* © Mark Richards/ PhotoEdit; *51 (left)* © David Young-Wolff/PhotoEdit; *(right)* © Walter Gilardetti; *52* © Bob Daemmrich/ Stock, Boston; *53* © Superstock; *60* © Stuart Cohen; *71* © Walter Gilardetti; *72 (left)* © Walter Gilardetti; *(right)* © John Fung; *73 (top)* © Judy Gelles/Stock, Boston; *(middle)* © Walter Gilardetti; *(bottom left)* © Jean-Claude Lejeune; *(bottom right)* © Michael Newman/Photo Edit; *74* © Tony Freeman/ Photo Edit; *75* © Walter Gilardetti; *80* © Lisa Quinones/Black Star; *84* © Nik Wheeler; *91* © Walter Gilardetti; *93, (1)* © Peter Yates/SABA; *(2)* © Gary Wagner/Stock, Boston; *(3)* © Richard Pasley/Stock, Boston; *(4)* © David Ulmer/Stock, Boston; *(5)* © Walter Gilardetti; *(6)* © Walter Gilardetti, Courtesy Computer Learning Center, Somerville, MA; *95* Courtesy Lucas NovaSensor; *111* © Peter Menzel; *112 (top)* © Andy Freeberg; *(middle)* Courtesy of Amr Mohsen, Aptix Corporation, San Jose, CA; *(bottom)* © Jamie Tanaka; *113* © Courtesy of Pauline Lo Alker; *123* © Matthew Borkoski/Stock, Boston; *127* © John Fung; *128, (1), (3), (4)* © Walter Gilardetti; *(2)* © Bob Daemmrich/Stock, Boston; *129* © Beryl Goldberg; *131 (left)* © Peter Menzel/Stock, Boston; *(right)* © Jean-Claude Lejeune/Stock, Boston; *(bottom)* © Tim Barnwell; *134, 136* © Bob Daemmrich/Stock, Boston; *138* © Gerard Vandystadt/ Agence Vandystadt/Photo Researchers, Inc.; *149* © AP Photo/Bebeto Matthews; *150, (1)* © Wide World Photos, Inc.; *(2)* © 1988 Nelso Entertainment/Everett Collection; *(3)* © Robert Foothorap/Black Star; *(4)* © Alonso Marina Snopet/Time, Inc.; *(5)* © Ernst Haas; *(6)* © 1981 Universal City Studios Inc./ Everett Collection; *151, (7)* © John Loengard/Time Magazine; *(8)* © D. Kirkland/Sygma; *164* Murray Close/ © 1993 Universal City Studios Inc. and Amblin Entertainment; *169* © Jonathan Nourok/Photo Edit; *170, (1)* © Walter Gilardetti; *(2)* © Lou Dematteis/Jeroboam, Inc.; *(3)* © Gary Conner/Photo Edit; *(4)* © George Gerster/Comstock; *(5)* © Elizabeth Hamlin/Stock, Boston; *193* © Stephen Frisch/Stock, Boston; *194, (1)* © Michael J. Okoniewski/The Image Works; *(2)* © David Powers/Stock, Boston; *(3)* © Jack Spratt/The Image Works; *195, (4), (6)* © David Young-Wolff/Photo Edit; *(5)* © John Fung; *217* © Dave Bahruff/ Stock, Boston; *218, (1)* © Patrick Ward/Stock, Boston; *(2)* © Peter Menzel/Stock, Boston; *(3)* © David Young-Wolff/Photo Edit; *219, (4)* © Ellis Herwig/Stock, Boston; *(5)* © Ira Kirschenbaum/Stock, Boston; *(6)* © Bill Preston

Contents

CHAPTER two

CHAPTER three

CHAPTER four

CHAPTER five

CHAPTER eight

CHAPTER nine

CHAPTER ten

Crime and Punishment 193

CHAPTER eleven

The Physical World 217

CHAPTER twelve

Together on a Small Planet 237

Preface
the Third Edition

The Mosaic O... Program

The Mosaic One Program consists of fou... d a variety of supplemental materials for intermediate to high-intermedi... nts seeking to improve their English language skills. Each of the four texts ... rogram is carefully organized by chapter theme, vocabulary, gramm... ures, and where possible, language functions. As a result, informat... duced in a chapter of any one of the Mosaic One texts corresponds to and ... es material taught in the same chapter of the other three books, creating a tru... grated, four-skills approach.

The Mosaic One program is highly flexible. The texts in ... series may be used together or separately, depending on students' needs and ... goals. The books in this program include:

- **A Content-Based Grammar.** Designed to teach grammar through content, this book introduces, practices, and applies grammatical structures through the development of high-interest chapter topics. This thematic approach gives students motivation because they are improving their mastery of grammatical structures and vocabulary while expanding their own knowledge.
- **A Content-Based Writing Book.** This book takes students step-by-step through the writing process—from formulating ideas through the revision stage. Writing assignments progress from paragraphs to essays, and students write about interesting, contemporary subjects from the sciences, social sciences, and humanities that are relevant to their current or future academic coursework.
- **A Listening/Speaking Skills Book.** This book teaches study skills and language functions while maintaining a strong focus on both listening and speaking. Each chapter includes a realistic listening passage about an interesting topic related to the chapter theme. Short conversations also provide comprehension practice, and a variety of speaking activities reinforce use in context of language functions.
- **A Reading Skills Book.** The selections in this book help students develop their reading skills in a meaningful rather than a mechanical way—enabling them to successfully tackle other academic texts. The three readings per chapter are from a variety of authentic sources, such as textbooks, magazines, newspapers, and interviews, and are accompanied by pre- and postreading exercises, including skimming, scanning, making inferences, paraphrasing, and group problem solving.

Supp... ...ental Materials

In additior ...core texts outlined above, various supplemental materials are avail... ...t users of the third edition, including:

Ins... ...or's Manual

Ext... ...revised for the new edition, this manual provides instructions and g... for using the four core texts separately or in various combinations to ...cular program needs. For each of the core texts, there is a separate ...l with teaching tips, additional activities, and other suggestions. The ...ng materials have been greatly expanded in this edition.

Audio Program for Mosaic One: A Listening/Speaking Skills Book

Completely rerecorded for the new edition, the audio program is designed to be used in conjunction with those exercises that are indicated with a cassette icon in the student text. Complete tapescripts for all exercises are now included in the back of the student text.

Audio Program to Accompany Mosaic One: A Reading Skills Book

This new optional audio program contains selected readings from the student text. These taped selections of poems, articles, stories, and speeches enable students to listen at their leisure to the natural oral discourse of native readers for intonation and modeling. Readings that are included in this program are indicated with a cassette icon in the student text.

Video/Video Guide

New to this edition, the video program for Mosaic One contains authentic TV segments coordinated with the twelve chapter themes in the four texts. A variety of pre- and postviewing exercises and activities for this video are available in a separate Video Guide.

Mosaic One: A Content-Based Writing Book, Third Edition

Rationale

An effective writing course for nonnative speakers should develop independent writers through a systematic approach to the writing process. This process trains students to:

- generate and develop ideas
- learn language directly related to the topic
- apply the appropriate rhetorical patterns to a specific writing task
- evaluate and revise initial drafts of their work

Mosaic One: A Content-Based Writing Book, third edition, focuses on these crucial elements of the writing process.

Chapter Organization

Each chapter is divided into four parts. The first part, Ideas for Writing, helps students generate and develop ideas for writing about topics related to the theme of the chapter. Students achieve this goal through activities that include reacting to photographs, freewriting about strong opinions or previous experience, reading current articles or book excerpts for ideas, conducting research and interviews, and participating in interactive class activities.

The second part of the chapter, Language for Writing, presents words, expressions, and structures that students need to know and review in order to write about the chapter topic. Through a series of exercises, students practice these elements in context so that they can integrate them into their own writing.

The third part, Systems for Writing, introduces rhetorical patterns that give students the framework for expressing their ideas, presenting the format that the academic writing requires. This section includes explanations, models, and exercises.

The last part, Evaluating for Rewriting, guides students through a series of revisions that emphasize the importance of rewriting and helps students improve their own work. Each evaluation focuses on the particular teaching points of the chapter.

Mosaic One: A Content-Based Writing Book, third edition, is to be used sequentially, as new teaching points build on what was taught previously. However, teachers can reorder chapters if they wish, making minor adjustments to the review points. Each chapter covers three to five class hours, making the course well-suited to the typical academic semester or quarter.

New to the Third Edition

Mosaic One: A Content-Based Writing Book, third edition, remains dedicated to the task of developing independent writers and thinkers by guiding students through the elements of the writing process as outlined above. However, each chapter of the third edition contains new features and changes that make the text more timely and functional, including:

1. **Streamlined Design.** The two-color design and revised art program make this edition more appealing to today's students. The book is also more user-friendly because many directions have been shortened and clarified, exercises and activities have been numbered, and key information has been highlighted in shaded boxes and charts.

2. **New Chapter Theme on Crime and Punishment.** The third edition has an entirely new theme for Chapter Ten: Crime and Punishment. In addition, themes for several other chapters have been broadened to include new content.
3. **Thinking Critically.** This entirely new boxed feature appears in every chapter. It introduces students to higher-order thinking skills related to the reading selection in Part One.
4. **Focus on Testing.** Also appearing in each chapter, these new boxed features help students apply the teaching points in Part Three to an on-demand writing assignment.

In addition, specific changes in each section of a typical chapter are as follows:

- **Part One: Ideas for Writing.** Most of the reading selections have been updated or changed, making them more uniform in length and level of difficulty. Moreover, the readings in the beginning chapters have been made easier to read in order to make the transition from *Interactions Two: A Writing Process Book*, third edition, smoother.
- **Part Two: Language for Writing.** The structures and vocabulary required for the writing tasks in each chapter are still presented.
- **Part Three: Systems for Writing.** The students' options have been broadened by presenting more ways to write an essay. In addition, the teaching points have been streamlined and highlighted, making them easier to preview and review.
- **Part Four: Evaluating for Rewriting.** This component has been redesigned so it is easier to use.

Acknowledgments

Our thanks to the following reviewers whose comments, both favorable and critical, were of great value in the development of the third edition of the Interactions/Mosaic series:

Jean Al-Sibai, University of North Carolina; Janet Alexander, Waterbury College; Roberta Alexander, San Diego City College; Julie Alpert, Santa Barbara City College; Anita Cook, Tidewater Community College; Anne Deal Beavers, Heald Business College; Larry Berking, Monroe Community College; Deborah Busch, Delaware County Community College; Patricia A. Card, Chaminade University of Honolulu; José A. Carmona, Hudson County Community College; Kathleen Carroll, Fontbonne College; Consuela Chase, Loyola University; Lee Chen, California State University; Karen Cheng, University of Malaya; Gaye Childress, University of North Texas; Maria Conforti, University of Colorado; Earsie A. de Feliz, Arkansas State University; Elizabeth Devlin-Foltz, Montgomery County Adult Education; Colleen Dick, San Francisco Institute of English; Marta Dmytrenko-Ahrabian, Wayne State University; Margo Duffy, Northeast Wisconsin Technical; Magali Duignan, Augusta College; Janet Dyar, Meridian Community College; Anne Ediger, San Diego City College;

D. Frangie, Wayne State University; Robert Geryk, Wayne State University; Jeanne Gibson, American Language Academy; Kathleen Walsh Greene, Rhode Island College; Myra Harada, San Diego Mesa College; Kristin Hathhorn, Eastern Washington University; Mary Herbert, University of California-Davis; Joyce Homick, Houston Community College; Catherine Hutcheson, Texas Christian University; Suzie Johnston, Tyler Junior College; Donna Kauffman, Radford University; Emmie Lim, Cypress College; Patricia Mascarenas, Monte Vista Community School; Mark Mattison, Donnelly College; Diane Peak, Choate Rosemary Hall; James Pedersen, Irvine Valley College; Linda Quillan, Arkansas State University; Marnie Ramker, University of Illinois; Joan Roberts, The Doane Stuart School; Doralee Robertson, Jacksonville University; Ellen Rosen, Fullerton College; Jean Sawyer, American Language Academy; Frances Schulze, College of San Mateo; Sherrie R. Sellers, Brigham Young University; Tess M. Shafer, Edmonds Community College; Heinz F. Tengler, Lado International College; Sara Tipton, Wayne State University; Karen R. Vallejo, Brigham Young University; Susan Williams, University of Central Florida; Mary Shepard Wong, El Camino College; Cindy Yoder, Eastern Mennonite College; Cheryl L. Youtsey, Loyola University; Miriam Zahler, Wayne State University; Maria Zien, English Center, Miami; Yongmin Zhu, Los Medanos College; Norma Zorilla, Fresno Pacific College.

Summary of Writing Skills and Activities

Chapter	Part One: Prewriting Activities	Part Two: Grammar and Vocabulary
one	• describe and compare cultures • freewrite • read a letter from a friend	• describing impressions • describing problems • asking information questions
two	• identify opposing points of view • freewrite • read an essay on education	• discussing issues in education • discussing advantages/ disadvantages
three	• describe/compare family relationships • freewrite • read an interview of a family member	• describing roles • describing relationships
four	• discuss lifestyle and causes/ effects of good/poor health • freewrite • read a news article about a health issue	• showing causes/effects • describing influences on health
five	• discuss advantages/ disadvantages of technology • freewrite • read a magazine article about micromachines	• discussing technology • using quotations • paraphrasing
six	• discuss success in business • freewrite • read a news article about successful immigrants in business	• discussing success in business

Part Three: Rhetorical and Stylistic Conventions	Part Four: Revision and Editing Skills	Additional Activities
• the paragraph • the topic sentence	• edit for topic sentence and revise	• interview a classmate • practice focusing your paragraphs
• paragraph unity • paragraph organization	• edit for paragraph unity/ organization and revise	• take a survey • practice editing
• from paragraph to essay	• edit for essay form/content and revise	• interview an American • make an outline
• the thesis statement	• edit for thesis statement and revise	• interview five Americans and use a chart to record results • practice writing under pressure
• essay introductions • essay development	• edit for introduction/thesis statement/supporting ideas and revise	• make predictions about technology • do library research
• paragraph coherence • essay conclusions	• edit for coherence and revise	• do library research • practice paraphrasing

Summary of Writing Skills and Activities

Chapter	Part One: Prewriting Activities	Part Two: Grammar and Vocabulary
seven	• categorize leisure-time activities • freewrite • read about the Olympic games	• classifying leisure-time activities • reviewing countable/ noncountable nouns
eight	• discuss factors that contribute to creativity • freewrite • read an essay on creativity	• making comparisons • describing the creative process
nine	• discuss/list examples of nonverbal behavior • read an excerpt from a textbook on nonverbal behavior	• describing nonverbal behavior and cultural values • interpreting nonverbal behavior
ten	• agree/disagree with statements about crime • freewrite • read a magazine essay on crime and punishment	• citing authorities • exposing weaknesses in opposing arguments
eleven	• compare different environments and cultures • freewrite • read a book excerpt on Inuit culture	• describing environmental conditions
twelve	• discuss intelligence • freewrite • read an essay on intelligence	• discussing intelligence • writing definitions

Part Three: Rhetorical and Stylistic Conventions	Part Four: Revision and Editing Skills	Additional Activities
• well-developed paragraphs	• edit for idea development and revise	• interview two people • develop a "bare bones" approach
• paragraph coherence: listing signals and sentence connectors • comparison paragraph organization	• edit for unity/organization/coherence/details and revise	• do research • practice revising
• paragraph development: patterns of organization • prepare an outline	• edit for pattern of organization and revise	• teach classmates a nonverbal behavior from your culture • watch a TV show and record nonverbal behavior
• summarize • summary-and-reaction essay organization	• edit for unity/organization/coherence/details and revise	• hold a debate
• sensory details	• edit for development/details and revise	• collect information on environment and culture
• essay organization: patterns of essay organization	• make your own editing questionnaire	• do research

CHAPTER one

New Challenges

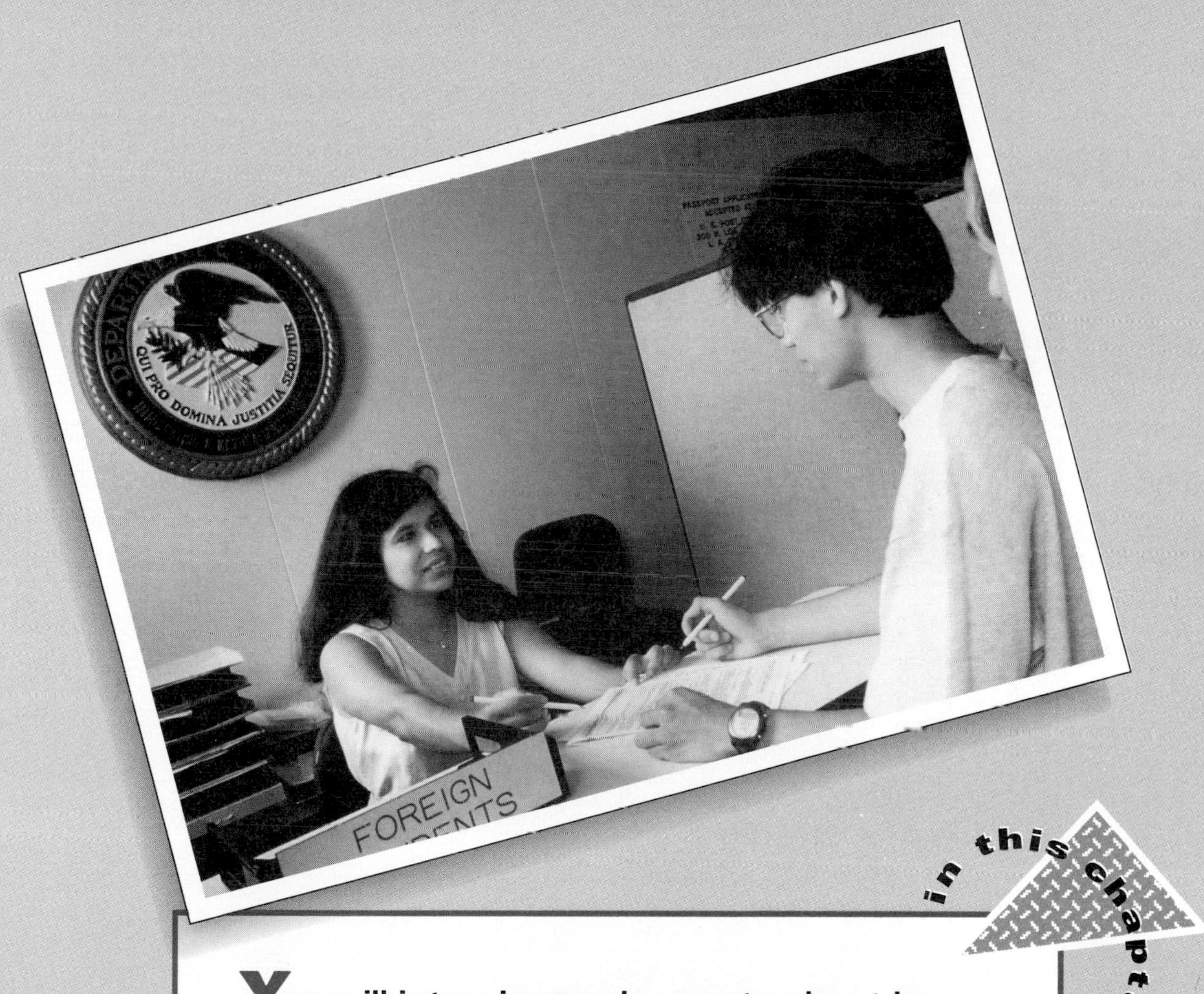

in this chapter

You will interview a classmate about her or his experiences adjusting to life in a new culture, and you will write about your own impressions and experiences of living in another culture.

PART one
Ideas for Writing

Getting Started

First impressions are important, especially when people visit a different country and get to know a new culture. What first impressions do people have of your home country? What are (or were) your first impressions of where you live now?

Look at the following photos of typical American scenes and describe what you see. Share your descriptions with your classmates. The first one is done as an example.

1. Media: TV is important in the United States. People get lots of information from TV.

2. Food: ______

3. Family: ______________________

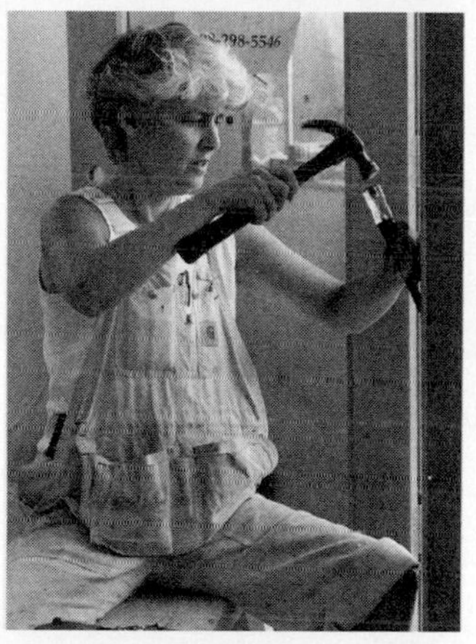

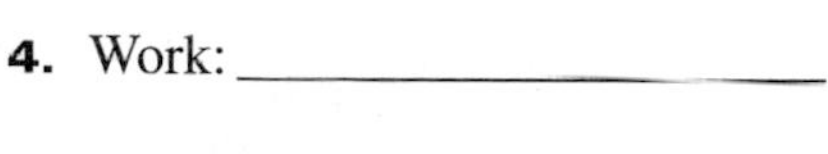

4. Work: ______________________

5. Education: ______________________

6. Health and fitness: ______________________

Brainstorming

Look again at the photos on pages 2 and 3 and compare American life to life in your culture or your country. Jot down your ideas below.

	AMERICAN CULTURE	MY CULTURE
1.	TV has a lot of influence in the United States.	Fewer people watch TV (and believe what they see on TV) in my country.
2.		
3.		
4.		
5.		
6.		

Freewriting

What were your first impressions of the place where you live now? What were some of the things that surprised you? What was difficult? Write for five minutes without stopping.

Reading for Ideas

David Vega has gone to Japan to teach English. He has written a letter to his Japanese-American friend in California, Alex Hirabayashi. Answer the following questions before you read what David writes from Tokyo.

prereading questions

1. What do you know about Tokyo? Share what you know with your classmates.
2. How would you or another student from your country react to Tokyo?
3. What do you think an American's reactions to Tokyo would be?

A Letter to Alex

Tokyo
September 30

Dear Alex,

Thanks for your card. Sorry I haven't written sooner. I've been spending all my free time wandering around Tokyo and learning about Japanese customs. It is very interesting here because everything is so different.

You asked me to write about some of the things I've noticed that are new to me. The most striking thing is the huge crowds. There are many, many people everywhere, but I have noticed that everyone is very orderly and polite. People at home would not be so orderly in such crowded conditions. Another new thing for me is the way the food is displayed in restaurant windows. It is very beautifully arranged on lacquer trays in simple, clean designs. The appearance of food in Japan seems to be as important as the taste. I've tried sushi several times and it was more delicious than at home. (The wasabi* was so strong I couldn't eat it.)

There are a few things that I've had trouble with since I arrived. Everything is written in Japanese, and even though your mother taught me a few Japanese characters before I left, I can't read a thing. Since I can't read signs, it is difficult to travel around. Most people are friendly, but they can't help me much because they don't speak English. Another difficulty is the Japanese public restrooms. Nobody warned me that the toilets are not like our Western ones—that has taken some adjusting!

Well, that's about all for now. I hope I'll understand more Japanese when I write you next time. I think things will get easier when I start teaching. Please give my regards to your family. Write back soon.

Take care,
David

---

* Wasabi is an Asian plant, the root of which is used to flavor food.

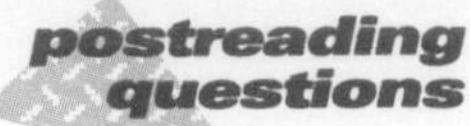

1. What are some things David likes about Tokyo? ____________________

____

____

2. What are two things David notices about the food in Japan?

____

____

3. What does David find difficult? Why? What was something that was difficult for you when you first arrived in Canada or the United States?

____

____

4. David is planning to stay in Tokyo for one year. What kinds of things do you think he will do and learn during the year? How do you think he'll feel at the end of the year? Do some predicting. ____________________

____

____

5. Each paragraph of David's letter contains one main idea. Make an outline of David's letter, listing the topic of each paragraph. ____________________

____

____

____

____

THINKING CRITICALLY

Making Inferences

Use what you know from David's letter to make guesses about what you don't know. This is called *inferring,* and it is an important critical thinking skill.

1. **Which of the following statements can be inferred from David's letter? Which cannot? Explain your choices.**
   a. **David can speak Japanese.**
   b. **David plans to study Japanese in Japan.**
   c. **David learned some Japanese from Alex's mother.**
   d. **Alex speaks fluent Japanese.**
2. **Why do you think David finds the sushi in Japan "more delicious" than the sushi he ate in California? Can you find food from your country where you live now? Is it as delicious as the same food when you eat it at home? Why or why not?**

Discuss the answers to these questions with your classmates.

Gathering Information

Now tell a classmate about your experiences adjusting to a new culture. You can talk about where you live now or about another place you visited. Talk about language, making friends, food, and taking care of day-to-day business. Your classmate will take notes on what you say.

ADJUSTING TO A NEW CULTURE

Classmate's Name: ______________________

New Culture: ______________________

Year: ______________________

First Impressions: ______________________

Difficulties: ______________________

Language for Writing

Describing Impressions of People, Places, and Things

David's letter gives the reader a good picture of his first impressions of Tokyo because he uses specific details. Review the words David used, which are listed in the chart below. Then add some words and expressions that describe the impressions of people, places, and things you had when you first arrived at where you now live.

	people	places	things
David in Tokyo	–very orderly and polite –friendly, but don't speak English	–many, many people everywhere –signs all in Japanese –public restrooms not like our Western ones	–food is beautifully arranged –sushi is more delicious than at home –wasabi is so strong I couldn't eat it
You in ________			

Describing Problems

Study the expressions below that David used to describe his problems adjusting to life in Tokyo. Use them as the basis for writing sentences about your own problems adjusting to life in a new culture. Share your sentences with your classmates when you're finished.

The noun was so adjective I couldn't verb (it).

I've had trouble with noun.

I can't verb.

They can't help me much because they don't verb.

Not being able to verb makes it difficult to verb.

The other difficulty is the noun.

Nobody warned me that the noun verb (not) like noun.

I think things will get easier when I start verb-ing.

Asking Information Questions

Asking information questions is one way to learn about a new culture and make new friends. These questions ask for more information than a *yes* or *no* answer.

Make a list of information questions that you might want to ask someone who has arrived here recently. Write as many questions as you can for each item. When you finish, share your list with your classmates.

1. What . . . ?

2. When . . . ?

3. Where . . . ?

4. How much . . . ?

5. How many . . . ?

6. How long . . . ?

7. Why . . . ?

Practicing What You've Learned

Using your best information questions from the previous exercise, interview a classmate about his or her experiences adjusting to a new culture. Since the answers to your questions will include lots of specific details, you can interview the same person you worked with in Part One, or you can work with a new partner. Record your results in the following chart.

ADJUSTING TO A NEW CULTURE

Classmate's Name: ______________________

New Culture: ______________________

Year: ______________________

Questions	Answers

Make a list of the words and expressions your partner used to describe his or her impressions of a new culture. If necessary, refer to the list of David's words and expressions in Describing Impressions of People, Places, and Things.

Write at least one paragraph about your partner's experiences as a newcomer to this country based on information from your interview. If possible, organize the ideas into more than one paragraph, like David did in his letter.

Write at least one paragraph about your own problems adjusting to a new culture.

Write a paragraph about the positive discoveries you have made in a new culture. Use the words and expressions you have learned in this chapter.

PART **three**

Systems for Writing

The Paragraph

New Points

- A paragraph is a group of sentences that develops an idea.
- The sentences of a paragraph *support* and *give examples* of the main idea.
- A paragraph begins with an *indented* sentence.
- A paragraph can stand alone, or it can be grouped with other paragraphs to develop a more general idea, as in an essay.

THIS IS A PARAGRAPH:

You asked me to write about some of the things I've noticed that are new to me. The most striking thing is the huge crowds. There are many, many people everywhere, but I have noticed that everyone is very orderly and polite. People at home would not be so orderly in such crowded conditions. Another new thing for me is the way the food is displayed in restaurant windows. It is very beautifully arranged on lacquer trays in simple, clean designs. The appearance of food in Japan seems to be as important as the taste. I've tried sushi several times, and it was much more delicious than at home. (The wasabi was so strong I couldn't eat it.)

WHY?

- The first sentence is indented.
- There is a main idea: All the sentences are about things David has noticed in Tokyo.
- Each sentence is an example of something he has noticed.

THIS ISN'T A PARAGRAPH:

I went to the Grand Canyon this winter and to Mexico in the spring of 94. I visited Taxco and bought some silver jewelry. The trip reminded me of vacations when I was young because my family always visited interesting tourist spots. I really like to travel to different countries. And if I know the language of the country I'm visiting, I enjoy myself more, of course. I studied Spanish in high school, and now I'm studying English. Some day I hope to visit Australia.

WHY NOT?

- The first sentence is not indented.
- The sentences are about different topics: a trip to the Grand Canyon, a trip to Mexico, memories, travel, languages.
- There is no main idea.

The Topic Sentence

New Points

- A paragraph usually begins with a sentence that expresses the main idea. This is the topic sentence.
- The topic sentence contains only one main idea and it tells the reader what the paragraph is about.
- The topic sentence can also appear in the middle or at the end of a paragraph.

THIS IS A TOPIC SENTENCE:

There are a few things that I've had trouble with since I arrived.

WHY?

- It introduces one main idea: difficulties since David arrived in Japan.
- It tells the reader what the paragraph is about.

THIS ISN'T A TOPIC SENTENCE:

I went to the Grand Canyon this winter and to Mexico in the spring of 94.

WHY NOT?

- The first sentence includes more than one main idea.
- It does not tell the reader what the paragraph is about.

focus on testing

Focusing Your Paragraph

The preceding box points out the characteristics of a good topic sentence. When you write an essay under time pressure, make sure your topic sentence follows these guidelines. A good topic sentence will focus your writing and help the reader follow your ideas.

Practicing What You've Learned

The following three paragraphs discuss American cultural preferences about body contact, personal attractiveness, and social activities. Identify the topic sentence in each paragraph and underline it.

A. English speakers generally avoid body contact when they speak to each other. Usually, they will not even touch each other with their hands. When they have to stand close together—for example, in an elevator—their muscles are tense, they avoid looking directly at each other, and they are silent. Even husbands and wives generally do not touch in public.*

B. Every culture has its standards for personal attractiveness. Nigerians think plumpness is attractive, whereas Americans prefer slenderness. In France, a man looks attractive wearing a jacket over his shoulders, with his arms out of the sleeves; in America, the same man dressed this way would look feminine. People in some cultures like natural body smells; people in others, including Americans, do not.†

C. The emphasis Americans give to time in social activities seems extreme to some foreigners. Many Americans, for example, believe that church services should start at exactly 11:00 A.M. and end by 12:00; they do not permit ministers to preach too long. School dances must end at 10:00 P.M., even though the boys and girls are behaving themselves and having a wonderful time. Americans sometimes judge restaurants by the speed of their service, rather than the quality of their food.‡

Now exchange answers with a partner. Were the main ideas expressed in the same place in each paragraph?

Paragraphs A, B, and C need topic sentences. First, read each paragraph and on pages 15 and 16 list all the supporting ideas it contains. This will help you understand what each paragraph is about. Then, choose the best topic sentence from the three possibilities given, as in the example. Go over your answers in class.

---

* Adapted from Gregory A. Barnes, *Communication Skills for the Foreign-Born Professional* (Philadelphia: ISI Press, 1982), p. 11.

† Adapted from Barnes, *Communication Skills for the Foreign-Born Professional*, p. 13.

‡ Adapted from Barnes, *Communication Skills for the Foreign-Born Professional*, p. 10.

example: In fact, many Americans go to France specifically to sample its excellent cuisine. This is because the appearance and taste of French food are famous throughout the world, and the ingredients are not foreign to Americans. As a matter of fact, though many Americans have difficulty with the French language, they often know various French food terms, such as *pâté, soufflé, quiche,* and *croissant*. Although Americans visiting France may have a difficult time speaking French and making friends, they rarely have difficulty with the food.

SUPPORTING IDEAS

Americans go to France because of its cuisine. French cuisine isn't foreign to Americans. They know food terms. Even though they may have trouble with some aspects of French culture, they like the food.

TOPIC SENTENCES

1. Many Americans have difficulty adjusting to French culture.
2. Many Americans understand French food terms.
3. The one aspect of French culture that many Americans have little difficulty adjusting to is the cuisine.

A. In introductions as well as in general conversations, speakers maintain frequent eye contact. That is, they look directly at each other. Most people become nervous if there is too much eye contact: This is called *staring*. When shaking hands, people shake firmly and *briefly*. The expression "He shakes hands like a dead fish" refers to a limp or weak handshake, a sign in American culture of a weak character. Prolonged handshaking is not unusual.*

SUPPORTING IDEAS

____

____

____

TOPIC SENTENCES

1. Direct eye contact is important during introductions in the United States.
2. In America, limp handshakes are a sign of weak character.
3. Direct eye contact and firm handshakes during introductions are customary in the United States.

---

* Adapted from Deena R. Levine and Mara B. Adelman, *Beyond Language: Intercultural Communication for English as a Second Language* (Englewood Cliffs, NJ: Prentice-Hall. 1982).

B. A few days in the home of a friendly family can help the student make the change to a new environment. A host family can help the student learn about American customs and family life and social and cultural activities in the community. Most importantly, the host family can be friends in the community to which the student may turn to in the difficult period of cultural adjustment. The relationship may be equally valuable for the participating family. By hosting an international student, family members can increase their knowledge and awareness of another culture and country.*

SUPPORTING IDEAS

____

____

____

TOPIC SENTENCES

1. Arriving in a foreign country can be a lonely and bewildering time for a new student from abroad.
2. Because being a new foreign student can be a lonely and difficult experience, staying with a host family is helpful and comforting.
3. A host family can learn a great deal about foreign people and their cultures by offering hospitality to a foreign student.

C. The most common problem foreign students face in adjusting to a new culture is an "identity crisis." Foreign students must adapt their old selves to a new situation, and this results in personality changes. They may have to play a different role in this new environment. The identity crisis occurs when the student has to consider who she or he really is. The process can be difficult, but if the student is aware of this problem, she or he can usually overcome it.†

SUPPORTING IDEAS

____

____

____

TOPIC SENTENCES

1. When people move between cultures, certain problems of adaptation always occur.
2. There are many problems a foreign student faces when leaving his or her country, such as finding a place to live and learning the way around town.
3. People face problems throughout life, and a foreign student is no exception.

---

* Adapted from Jim Leonard, "Design for a One-Day Host Family Workshop," *Readings in Intercultural Communication* 5 (Pittsburgh, PA: The Intercultural Communications Network, 1976), p. 30.

† Adapted from Jerry Wilcox, James O'Driscoll, Nobleza Asuncion-Lande, and Cal Downs, "Models for Re-Entry Transition Seminars and Workshops," *Readings in Intercultural Communication* 5 (Pittsburgh, PA: The Intercultural Communications Network, 1976), p. 173

In this exercise, you will read three topic sentences. For each of these, predict what you would expect to read in the rest of the paragraph. Make notes about your predictions as in the example; then compare your notes with a partner's.

example: Most people live for a long time in a new culture before they can relax and accept what they see around them.

The new culture is different. The foreigner is nervous, intimidated, and confused at first. Examples: College registration procedures are bureaucratic, complicated. With time, one becomes accustomed to things, accepts them, and sees benefits.

1. Some very funny things happened to me during my first few days in the United States, but the most comical was our night in a Boston restaurant.

____
____
____
____
____

2. There are advantages and disadvantages to being a foreign or immigrant student.

____
____
____
____
____

3. Moving to another culture is often difficult because you usually do not have family and friends around for emotional support.

____
____
____
____
____

In this exercise, you are going to write topic sentences for the following three paragraphs. As you did in Exercise 2, make a list of all the supporting ideas in each paragraph before you write the topic sentence. Be sure your topic sentences have one main idea, have a clear focus, and tell the reader what the paragraph is about.

A. *Topic sentence:* ____________________

____

For example, North Americans do not prolong eye contact during a conversation, whereas South Americans do. A person from North America usually meets the other person's eyes for a few seconds, looks away, and then back again, but a South American looks directly into the other person's eyes and considers it impolite not to do so. Another difference is the contrast in using hand movements while speaking. The South American uses many gestures. The North American, however, uses them only occasionally. The North and South American have more in common when we examine the distance each maintains from the person he or she is talking with. Unless a close friendship exists, both the North and the South American stand about two to three feet from one another. By studying the differences in body language of a group of North and South Americans, we could probably figure out where each person comes from.*

SUPPORTING IDEAS

____

____

____

B. *Topic sentence:* ____________________

____

In Paris one can recognize Americans two hundred yards away simply by the way they walk. A French student told me that when he returned home after three months at the Harvard Business School, his father was shocked when he saw his son walk from the plane. "You've become an American," were his first words of greeting. "You bounce when you walk!" An American often walks with swinging arms and a rolling pelvis as though moving through a space unlimited by human or physical obstacles.†

SUPPORTING IDEAS

____

____

____

---

* Adapted from Wilcox et al., *Readings in Intercultural Communication* 5, p. 15.

† From Lawrence Wylie, *Beaux Gestes: A Guide to French Body Talk* (Cambridge, MA: The Undergraduate Press, 1977), p. xi.

C. *Topic sentence:* ______________________________

____

A common example is the gesture of waving farewell. In Italy the palm of the hand is held toward the speaker and the fingers make the motion of drawing the departing person back. In Spain the movement is the same, but the hand is held horizontally. In France, the palm is frequently held facing the departing person, and the movement of the hand appears to push the departing person on his way. Some scholars think that exposing one's palm indicates surrender, so perhaps the French form of farewell implies a reassurance of nonaggression. Americans are inclined to show the palm also and move the flattened hand from left to right.*

SUPPORTING IDEAS

____

____

____

While some writers create a topic sentence when they begin a paragraph, other writers write their topic sentence *after* deciding what their paragraph is about. For example, imagine that David has to write a paragraph about his first impressions of Tokyo, based on his letter on page 5. He wants to organize his ideas first, then write the topic sentence, then complete his paragraph. The steps here and on pages 20 to 22 will show you how to write a topic sentence this way, using David's paragraph as a model.

1. Make a list of all the things that impressed you when you first came to a new culture. Look at David's list, then make a list of your ideas.

DAVID'S LIST OF IMPRESSIONS OF JAPAN	YOUR LIST OF IMPRESSIONS OF ______
I read a few travel books about Japan before I went.	______
People are so busy.	______
Tokyo was so crowded.	______
People were orderly and polite.	______
Food was beautifully arranged.	______
I went to Nara and fed the deer.	______
The sushi was more delicious in Tokyo than at home.	______
	______
	______
	______

* Adapted from Wylie, *Beaux Gestes: A Guide to French Body Talk*, p. xii.

2. Look through the list for related ideas. This will help you find the main idea of your paragraph. Cross out any unrelated items.

DAVID'S LIST	YOUR LIST

I read a few travel books about Japan before I went.

People are so busy.
Tokyo was so crowded.
People were orderly and polite.
Food was beautifully arranged.

I went to Nara and fed the deer.
The sushi was more delicious in Tokyo than at home.

3. Now write a topic sentence that describes the main idea you found in step 2.

DAVID'S TOPIC SENTENCE	YOUR TOPIC SENTENCE
I've had lots of surprises since I arrived in Tokyo.	______________________

4. Exchange papers with a partner or with your teacher. Have your partner check to see that your topic sentence has a main idea and that it tells the reader what the paragraph is about. Note that David's first attempt at a topic sentence doesn't tell the reader what the rest of the paragraph is about. Look at his corrected topic sentence, then check yours.

DAVID'S TOPIC SENTENCE	YOUR TOPIC SENTENCE
There are some things about life in Tokyo that the newcomer will find different from life in the United States or Canada.	______________________

Japanese bullet train (left); Japanese steward "assisting" passengers onto train (right)

5. Complete the paragraph, remembering to include all the supporting ideas your topic sentence suggests. Include specific examples to develop your main idea.

DAVID'S FINAL PARAGRAPH

There are some things about life in Tokyo that the newcomer will find different from life in the United States or Canada. The most striking thing is the huge crowds. There are many, many people everywhere, but I have noticed that everyone is very orderly and polite. People at home would not be so orderly in such crowded conditions. Another new thing for me was the way the food is displayed in restaurant windows. It is very beautifully arranged on lacquer trays in simple, clean designs. The appearance of food in Japan seems to be as important as the taste. I've tried sushi several times, and it is more delicious than at home.

YOUR FINAL PARAGRAPH

____
____
____
____
____
____
____
____
____
____
____
____
____
____
____
____

Writing Assignments

Complete at least one of the following assignments. Use what you've learned from this chapter to make your writing interesting and clear.

1. Write a paragraph about your problems adjusting to life in the United States or Canada. Refer to the steps in developing a topic sentence to get you started.
2. Write about the positive discoveries you've made since you arrived in a new culture. Look at the second paragraph of David's letter to begin.
3. Combine assignments 1 and 2 into a letter to someone from your country. Describe both the positive and negative things you've found in the new culture. Share your letter with your classmates, then send it!
4. Write a paragraph about possible problems one could encounter adjusting to life in your country.

5. Choose one of the photographs from Part One and write a paragraph describing what it shows about American culture.
6. Write a paragraph describing your first impressions of the college or school you are currently attending.

7. Write a paragraph about any aspect of coming to a new culture that interests you.

PART four
Evaluating for Rewriting

An ongoing stage of writing is evaluating what you have written and rewriting it. The last section of each chapter will help you do this. First you will exchange papers and evaluate a classmate's writing. Then you will answer some questions about your own writing.

Working with Your Partner

Exchange the paragraphs you wrote for the Writing Assignments section. Use the following questionnaire to evaluate each other's paragraphs.

1. Read the topic sentence only. How many ideas does it express?

   One _____ More than one _____

2. Read the topic sentence again. What do you expect to read about in the paragraph? Write your ideas here:

   ____

   ____

   ____

3. Now read the paragraph. Were your predictions correct?

   Yes _____ No_____

4. Are there any irrelevant ideas in the paragraph (ideas that the topic sentence does not suggest)?

   Yes _____ No _____

   If Yes, underline the irrelevant sentences.

Return each other's paragraphs. Read your partner's evaluation of your paragraph. Discuss any questions you have with your partner.

Working on Your Own

Now you are ready to evaluate your own paragraph. Consider your partner's evaluation comments. Do you need to rewrite your topic sentence? Do you need to add more information? Do you need to eliminate any irrelevant information? What other changes, if any, do you need to make?

Rewrite your paragraph, making any necessary changes. Turn this revised draft of your paragraph in to your teacher.

CHAPTER two

Looking at Learning

in this chapter

You will interview people in and out of class about an issue in education and write about your own opinions on educational issues.

PART one
Ideas for Writing

Getting Started

Students have opinions on many subjects, but they are often the most interested about issues that affect them directly: issues in education. You and your classmates may be concerned about many of these issues at your school: Are lecture classes too large and impersonal? Is the atmosphere too competitive? Are your instructors really helping you learn? Are classes preparing you for a career?

Read the following statements by a variety of people who work and study at American colleges and universities.

1. *Gloria (third-year student):* "I like seminar classes best because I can really learn in a small class. Those huge lecture classes are a waste of time."
2. *David (second-year student):* "Although my parents want me to continue my education and get an advanced degree, I'm anxious to get a job and gain some work experience."

3. *Alice (college admissions officer):* "People shouldn't go to college with the idea that it guarantees them a job—there are plenty of people with college degrees who can't find work. You should go to college to become educated, for the love of learning."
4. *Eric (computer science major):* "I can't understand why I have to study English literature and world history. I won't need those courses to become a computer programmer."
5. *Karen (English major):* "I majored in the humanities because I thought I'd learn more about people and life than if I majored in biology or chemistry."
6. *Ted (faculty member):* "As a professor, I like to think of myself more as a consultant than an authority figure."
7. *Marta (foreign student adviser):* "There's still too much emphasis on European ideas and history in higher education. We need to expand the curriculum to include the literature, history, and traditions of all cultures."
8. *Bernard (foreign student):* "Learning is best when everyone helps each other out in a cooperative atmosphere."

Read the statements again with a classmate. For each one, decide what the opposing viewpoint is. Then record this information in the following chart. The first one is done as an example.

WHO SAID IT?	WHAT DID SHE OR HE SAY?	WHAT'S THE OPPOSING POINT OF VIEW?
Gloria	Seminars are better than lectures.	Lecture classes are better.

With one or two classmates, compare your charts. Do they match? List any additional issues you can think of on the lines below. You may want to add several issues in education from your home country.

____

____

____

Brainstorming

With a classmate, think of ideas that support each side of the issues in the chart above. Then record these notes in the spaces that follow. You will expand these points into sentences and paragraphs in the future assignments.

SEMINARS	VS.	LECTURES
• Students receive more personal attention. • Students can ask lots of questions. • Students work very hard.		• Instructors can cover lots of material in a short time. • Students learn good study habits. • Teaching assistants give extra help.
GETTING A JOB	**VS.**	**GOING TO COLLEGE**
______ ______ ______		______ ______ ______
EDUCATION FOR PERSONAL GROWTH	**VS.**	**EDUCATION FOR A JOB**
______ ______ ______		______ ______ ______
A VOCATIONAL EDUCATION	**VS.**	**LIBERAL ARTS EDUCATION**
______ ______ ______		______ ______ ______
THE HUMANITIES	**VS.**	**THE SCIENCES**
______ ______ ______		______ ______ ______

TEACHERS AS CONSULTANTS	VS.	TEACHERS AS AUTHORITIES
______________________		______________________
______________________		______________________
______________________		______________________

MULTICULTURAL CURRICULUM	VS.	EURO-CENTRIC CURRICULUM
______________________		______________________
______________________		______________________
______________________		______________________

COOPERATIVE LEARNING	VS.	COMPETITIVE LEARNING
______________________		______________________
______________________		______________________
______________________		______________________

Freewriting

Choose one of the issues in education you've been discussing—the issue that interests you most. Write about this issue for five minutes without stopping.

Reading for Ideas

You are going to read an article by Caroline Bird about whether or not all high school graduates should go to college. Before you read, answer the questions on page 30.

1. What are some reasons for going to college? Make a list with your classmates.

2. Why might a student decide *not* to go to college? Make another list of reasons for *not* going to college.

3. Does everyone in your country attend college? What is the attitude in your country toward people who don't attend college?

4. What do you think is the most important reason for attending college?

5. In your opinion, are there some valid reasons why a high school graduate would choose not to go to college? What would those reasons be?

Where College Fails Us

The case for college has been accepted without question for more than a generation. All high school graduates ought to go, say conventional wisdom and statistical evidence, because college will help them earn more money, become "better" people, and learn to be more responsible citizens than those who don't go.

But college has never been able to work its magic for everyone. And now that close to half our high school graduates are attending, those who don't fit the pattern are becoming more numerous, and more obvious. College graduates are selling shoes and driving taxis; college students sabotage each other's experiments and forge letters of recommendation in the intense competition for admission to graduate school. Others find no stimulation in their studies, and drop out—often encouraged by college administrators.

Some adventuresome educators and campus watchers have openly begun to suggest that college may not be the best, the proper, the only place for every young person after the completion of high school. Perhaps college doesn't make people intelligent, ambitious, happy, liberal, or quick to learn new things—maybe it's just the other way around, and intelligent, ambitious, happy, liberal, and quick-learning people are merely the ones who have been attracted to college in the first place. And perhaps all those successful college graduates would have been successful whether they had gone to college or not.

Students tell us the same thing college counselors tell us—they go because of pressure from parents and teachers, and stay because it seems to be an alternative to a far worse fate. It's "better" than the Army or a dead-end job, and it has to be pretty bad before it's any worse than staying at home. Potential college graduates say that they don't want to work "just" for the money: They want work that matters. They want to help people and save the world. But the numbers are stacked against them. Not only are there not enough jobs in the world-saving fields, but in the current slowdown it has become evident that there never were, and probably never will be, enough jobs requiring higher education to go around.

Whatever college graduates *want* to do, most of them are going to wind up doing what *there is* to do. During the next few years, according to the Labor Department, the biggest demand will be for the stenographers and secretaries, followed by retail-trade salesworkers, hospital attendants, bookkeepers, building custodians, registered nurses, foremen, kindergarten and elementary-school teachers, receptionists, cooks, cosmetologists, private-household workers, manufacturing inspectors, and industrial machinery repairmen. These are the jobs which will eventually absorb the surplus archaeologists, urban planners, oceanographers, sociologists, editors, and college professors. Students who have graduated in specialized fields often find that they have learned a lot of things in classrooms that they will never use. One disillusioned architecture student, who had already designed and built houses, said, "It's the degree you need, not everything you learn getting it."

What students and graduates say that they did learn on campus comes under the heading of personal, rather than intellectual, development. Again and again I was told that the real value of college is learning to get along with others, to practice social skills, to "sort out my head," and these have nothing to do with curriculum.

College is an ideal place for those young adults who love learning for its own sake, who would rather read than eat, and who like nothing better than writing research papers. But they are a minority, even at the prestigious colleges, which recruit and attract the intellectually oriented.

The rest of our high school graduates need to look at college more closely and critically, to examine it as a consumer product, and decide if the cost in dollars, in time, in continued dependency, and in future returns, is worth the very large investment each student—and family—must make.

Caroline Bird

1. According to the author, what is college "supposed" to do?

2. What are some reasons students give for attending college?

3. What does the author describe as the situation for students who have graduated from college?

4. Does the author believe all students should attend college? Why or why not?

5. Do you agree with the author of this article? Why or why not?

THINKING CRITICALLY

Analyzing Information

You are going to analyze the previous article, classify two types of Information contained in it, and then add your own ideas to the two classes. This kind of analysis is an important critical thinking skill.

1. **In the following chart, list the advantages and disadvantages of attending college. You may find some in the article, and you may have to think of your own.**

ADVANTAGES	DISADVANTAGES
______________________	______________________
______________________	______________________
______________________	______________________
______________________	______________________
______________________	______________________
______________________	______________________
______________________	______________________
______________________	______________________

2. **Discuss your list of advantages and disadvantages with your classmates.**

Gathering Information

Choose the statement from the ones made by the different people on pages 26 and 27 that most closely reflects your own point of view. State your point of view in a short sentence. Then make a questionnaire like the following one and write your point of view at the top. Ask two classmates and three native English speakers (out of class) to fill in the following questionnaire.

QUESTIONNAIRE

Statement (point of view) ______________________________

____

____

Name ______________________________

Age ______________________________

Male **Female** **(circle one)**

Occupation ______________________________

Do you agree or disagree with the statement above? __________

After you have finished the interview, write as many advantages as you can to the educational issue presented in the statement.

1. ______________________________

____

2. ______________________________

____

3. ______________________________

____

4. ______________________________

____

5. ______________________________

____

Language for Writing

Discussing Issues in Education

Caroline Bird uses the following expressions in "Where College Fails Us" on pages 30 to 32. Working in small groups, share your knowledge of the expressions by giving an explanation, a synonym, and/or an example for each.

1. to accept without question ____________________
2. conventional wisdom ____________________
3. to find stimulation in ____________________
4. a dead-end job ____________________
5. to be stacked against ____________________
6. to wind up ____________________
7. to come under the heading of ____________________
8. to "sort out my head" ____________________
9. a consumer product ____________________

Here and on the next page are some more words and expressions from Bird's article that are useful when writing about issues in education. Try to write a definition for each word or expression by studying it in context, that is, as it appears in Bird's article. If you still don't know the meaning, look it up in a dictionary.

NOUNS

graduates ____________________

admission ____________________

curriculum ____________________

graduate school ____________________

letters of recommendation ____________________

administrators ____________________

educators ____________________

degree ____________________

VERBS

graduate ______________________________

get along with ______________________________

recruit ______________________________

attract ______________________________

to be worth ______________________________

ADJECTIVES

ambitious ______________________________

liberal ______________________________

disillusioned ______________________________

intellectual ______________________________

prestigious ______________________________

Read these statements about the advantages and disadvantages of seminars and lectures and notice how the verbs in italics are used. If you don't know the meaning of a verb, look it up.

ADVANTAGES

Seminars . . .

1. *Encourage* close student-teacher relationships
2. *Enable* all the students in class to participate
3. *Provide* a more personal atmosphere
4. *Make it possible* for students to know each other

Lectures . . .

1. *Allow* students to take responsibility for their own learning
2. *Create* a formal learning setting
3. *Promote* independence and competition, which
4. *Prepare* students for life after graduation

DISADVANTAGES

Seminars . . .

1. *Lead* to a situation where there is too much contact between teachers and students
2. *Prevent* students from taking their studies seriously
3. *Allow* them to be lazy

Lectures . . .

1. *Inhibit* close relationships between students
2. *Discourage* real learning

Practicing What You've Learned

Write a short (one-paragraph) letter to Caroline Bird explaining your opinion on whether everyone should go to college. Use as many of her words and expressions as you can.

Read the following list of issues in education. Choose an issue. Write a paragraph about the advantages of one side of the issue. Then write a paragraph about the advantages of the other side of the same issue.

1. Education for professional training versus education for self-fulfillment
2. Humanities versus the sciences
3. Broad education versus specialization
4. Teacher as consultant versus teacher as authority figure
5. Cooperative learning versus competitive learning

Follow the instructions for Exercise 2, but this time focus on the disadvantages of both sides of the issue.

Write a paragraph on the advantages of seminars. Include specific examples that demonstrate why seminars are good. Refer to the statements on page 36.

Write a paragraph about the advantages of lectures. Refer to the statements on page 36 and, if possible, to your own experience.

PART three

Systems for Writing

Review Points

- Every paragraph has a topic sentence.
- The topic sentence tells the reader what the paragraph is about.

Paragraph Unity

New Points

- A paragraph has *unity* when all of its sentences relate to and develop the topic sentence.
- Having unity makes your paragraph easier to read.

Read the following paragraphs. Which one is a better example of a unified paragraph?

A. Studies have shown that community college students tend to learn more in introductory courses than students at four-year colleges. There are many reasons for this. One is that introductory humanities and science courses such as psychology and biology are usually much smaller at community colleges than at the typical four-year college. As a result, community college students often get more attention from their instructors. Another reason more real learning may take place in community college courses is that the instructors tend to be more dedicated to teaching: They are not required to do research and to publish books and articles as are tenured four-year college professors. Consequently, they have more time to devote to preparing lessons, grading papers, and meeting with students. These are just a few of the reasons that community college students often learn more than their counterparts at four-year colleges.

B. Most schools and colleges have counseling services that help students choose the appropriate courses for their majors and plan their careers. The services usually consist of counselors who see students individually or in small groups. In individual or group sessions, students, with the aid of a trained counselor, determine their academic and career goals. These services also provide aptitude, interest, personality, and achievement tests to help students learn more about their interests and abilities. There are also psychologists and therapists who help students with particular difficulties such as emotional disturbances or learning problems. In addition, health examinations as well as nursing and medical services are available in most schools. Therefore, students at most schools and colleges have many resources to help them make important academic and career choices.

Paragraph A is an example of a unified paragraph. Paragraph B isn't unified. Do you know why? In paragraph B, there are sentences that have nothing to do with the idea expressed in the topic sentence. In paragraph A, every sentence is related to the topic sentence.

focus on testing

Unifying Your Paragraphs

When you write an essay in a test situation, make sure that every sentence relates to or develops the topic sentence in each paragraph. Writing unified paragraphs will help the reader follow your ideas and make your essay easier to read.

Paragraph Organization

New Points

- Paragraph organization means putting all the sentences of a paragraph in a logical order.
- There are many different ways to organize ideas in a paragraph. The order you choose usually depends on the topic of the paragraph.

An outline of a well-organized paragraph might look like this:

I.	Topic sentence:	States your main idea
II.	Bridge:	Says more about your main idea or leads into your examples (optional)
III.	Examples:	Support your main idea with examples, facts, details, etc.
	A. Example 1	
	B. Example 2	
	C. Example 3, etc.	
IV.	Restatement:	Restates your main idea

Practice recognizing the parts of a well-organized paragraph by reading the paragraphs here and on page 40 and answering the questions that follow.

A. Colleges and universities in the United States and Canada offer a wide variety of subjects. Students can sample different fields of knowledge, but usually major (concentrate) in one field during the last two years of college. If they wish, they may obtain professional training at the undergraduate level—for example, in accounting, teaching, journalism, or chemistry. Certain colleges specialize in training agricultural experts and engineers. For those who wish to prepare for careers in the arts, there are private music schools and fine arts academies. These examples illustrate the variety of courses open to American college and university students.*

1. Where is the topic sentence? Underline it. Does it contain the main idea?
2. Is there an explanatory sentence (bridge) that follows it?
3. How many examples are there in the paragraph?
4. Does the last sentence in the paragraph restate the main idea?

B. A college community often offers more than classes—it can be a lively center of activities and organizations. Students participate in many different activities—social, religious, political, and athletic. Among the activities are college newspapers, musical organizations, dramatic clubs, and political groups. Some of these have faculty advisors. Many religious groups have their own meeting places where they hold services and social activities. Student groups plan activities of all types—from formal dances to picnics. Most colleges have a student union where students can get together for lunch, study sessions, club meetings, and socializing. It's easy to see that North American college students do much more than just study.†

1. What is the main idea of the paragraph? Where is it expressed?
2. What is the purpose of the second sentence in the paragraph?
3. What are the purposes of the third, fourth, fifth, sixth, and seventh sentences in the paragraph? How does the information in these sentences relate to the main idea?
4. What is the purpose of the last sentence in the paragraph?

Practicing What You've Learned

Practice what you've learned about paragraph unity and organization by editing the following paragraphs. Read each one carefully. First, find the main idea as expressed in the topic sentence. Then cross out any irrelevant sentences in the paragraphs.

A. (1) Many college and university students in the United States find it necessary to work while attending school in order to support themselves and pay tuition. (2) Some students qualify for "work-study" grants. (3) These are paid positions offered by the college or university to students who demonstrate financial need. (4) Work-study grants are often for positions in the school cafeteria or library. (5) A variety of grants and scholarships are available to qualified applicants from families that could not otherwise

* Adapted from Ethel Tiersky and Martin Tiersky, *Customs and Institutions: A Survey of American Culture and Traditions* (New York: Regents Publishing Co., 1975), pp. 155–156.

† Adapted from Tiersky and Tiersky, *Customs and Institutions: A Survey of American Culture and Traditions*, p. 157.

afford to provide a college education. (6) Other students whose family income may be too high to qualify for work-study grants have to find part-time jobs on their own in the community. (7) Although part-time work puts extra pressure on college students, many report that the experience actually helps them deal with academic demands.

B. (1) Many students in the United States live away from home while attending college. (2) In some cases, students choose colleges that are many miles away from their home town; some even go to schools on the other side of the country. (3) In this case, they must live apart from their families. (4) Some young people choose to leave home at the age of eighteen even though they are not attending college. (5) Even students who attend colleges in their own towns may sometimes decide to live in apartments or dormitories on campus. (6) Reasonably priced housing has become increasingly hard to find in many college communities. (7) Students who choose to live on campus rather than at home often do so because they want to be involved in campus activities. (8) Some also feel that living close to campus makes them study harder because they are away from the distractions of home life. (9) In general, it is more common for American college students to live on campus than at home.

C. (1) College education not only is a stepping stone toward any competitive profession, it also provides for a well-rounded life. (2) College provides all the general skills that can be applied to any profession. (3) In addition to preparing students for their future careers, studying at college helps students develop skills and interests they will find useful and important in the future. (4) Regardless of one's major, studying at college trains one's thinking and develops self-discipline. (5) People must exercise self-discipline throughout their lives: after graduation, with their marriage partners, and later as parents. (6) For example, studying Latin may not apply directly to one's career, but such study disciplines the mind and improves the memory. (7) Concepts learned in psychology courses can be useful in everything from childrearing to business management. (8) Music classes teach aesthetics and history. (9) Therefore, having a strong foundation in education can improve one's chances for a good job and develop life skills.

Read the following paragraphs. Decide which paragraphs are well-organized and which are not. Put a ✓ next to the letter of each well-organized paragraph. Refer to the outline of a well-organized paragraph on page 39 if you need help.

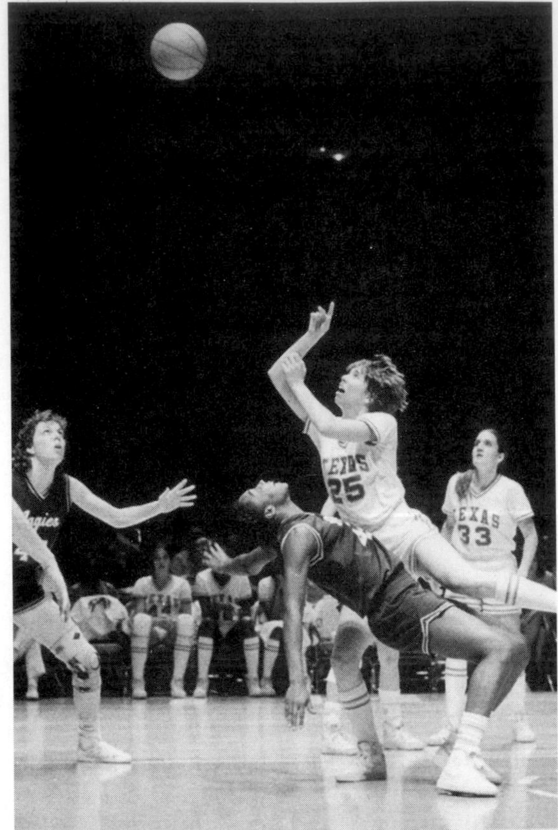

A. (1) Athletics is an important part of life on most American campuses. (2) In addition to required physical education courses, there are voluntary programs for health, recreation, and the development of teams for intercollegiate competition. (3) Most coeducational schools belong to an athletic league. (4) The teams within the league play against one another, aiming for the league championship. (5) Football is the college sport that stirs up the most national interest. (6) At large schools, promoting football, developing a team, and playing before huge crowds have become a big business. (7) People buy season tickets for substantial prices. (8) Games, complete with student marching bands and entertainment, are large productions. (9) Other sports—particularly basketball, swimming, and track—are also popular. (10) Some schools also have competitive tennis, skiing, sailing, wrestling, soccer, and baseball. (11) Indeed, sports play a significant role in American college life.*

B. (1) The schools of a particular society or country usually pass along the accepted customs, ideas, and beliefs of that society. (2) Through the years, schools have had several important aims. (3) These include (a) acquisition of knowledge, (b) intellectual discipline, (c) education for citizenship, (d) individual development, (e) vocational training, and (f) character education.†

C. (1) When a person's behavior changes, he has learned something. (2) He may learn outside of schools as well as in school. (3) A child may learn words and sentences so that he can communicate with others. (4) A person

---

* Adapted from *World Book Encyclopedia* (Chicago: Field Enterprises Educational Corp., 1962), pp. 56–58.

† Adapted from Tiersky and Tiersky, *Customs and Institutions: A Survey of American Culture and Traditions*, p. 158.

may learn to walk, to run, to jump, or to handle tools and operate a machine. (5) He may learn attitudes of liking and disliking and loving or hating. (6) He may learn to deal with other persons courteously and fairly or rudely and violently. (7) So no matter what he learns, the process involves changing behavior.*

For each paragraph that was not well organized in Exercise 2 (you probably found one), say which part was missing (the topic sentence, the examples, the restatement). Fix the paragraph by adding the missing parts.

Read the following notes from a class discussion about education at American universities. Then use the notes to write a well-organized paragraph with all the necessary elements—topic sentence, bridge (optional), examples, and restatement. Since the notes suggest more than one main idea, you must choose a unifying theme for your paragraph and eliminate all unrelated ideas. Feel free to add information based on your knowledge and experience. First, complete the chart below and on page 44 following the notes to help you organize your ideas.

- Students very competitive at large U.S. universities.
- Professors have many tricks to prevent cheating.
- High failure rate at large American universities.
- Exam questions switched at the last minute.
- Professors supply test booklets; students cannot use their own.
- Monitors patrol large exam halls.
- Students sit far away from each other.
- Cheating is a cause for dismissal from most U.S. universities.
- At large U.S. universities, you rarely see students comparing grades, sharing notes, or forming study groups, especially at the undergraduate level.
- Extremely difficult introductory courses eliminate a certain percentage of undergraduates from popular majors.

Topic sentence: ____

____

____

Bridge (optional): ____

____

Example 1: ____

____

____

* Adapted from *World Book Encyclopedia.*

Example 2: ____

____

____

Example 3: ____

____

____

Example 4: ____

____

____

Restatement: ____

____

____

____

Here's a similar activity. This class discussed the purpose of higher education. Some students thought the purpose of education is for personal enrichment and growth. Others believed that the only reason to pursue higher education is to prepare for a profession. Here are some notes from the discussion. Read them and follow the same procedure as you did in Exercise 4. You can write about one side of the issue or the other, or both sides. You may have to add information.

- A college education, regardless of one's major, trains one to think; it disciplines the mind.
- Studying Latin may not lead directly to a career, but it disciplines the mind and improves the memory.
- Students learn general skills in college that they can apply to any profession.
- There is a lot of competition for good jobs in the real world; you should prepare for this by getting a good education in your chosen field.
- Students who do not prepare for a career while in college are wasting time and money.
- Focusing on a career while in college is a waste of time because it is impossible to predict the future job market and economy.
- Psychology courses can be useful in everything from childrearing to business management.
- You can study languages, literature, and music in your free time, *after* you've gotten a good job.
- A business major is more likely to get a good job after graduation than an art history major.

Topic sentence: ____

____

____

Bridge (optional): ____

____

Example 1: ____

____

____

Example 2: ____

____

____

Example 3: ____

____

____

Example 4: ____

____

____

Restatement: ____

____

____

____

Writing Assignments

Write a paragraph on one of the following topics. Use the vocabulary and expressions you learned in this chapter. Make sure that your paragraph is unified and well-organized. Develop your ideas by using information from the research you did in Part One.

1. Write a paragraph in which you show the advantages or disadvantages of one of the following issues in education:

a. Small classes versus large ones
b. Majoring in the humanities versus majoring in science
c. Pursuing an education for professional training versus pursuing a career for self-fulfillment
d. Cooperation versus competition among students
e. Professors as authority figures versus professors as consultants

2. Write one or more paragraphs in which you compare a school or college in your country with one in the United States or Canada. You can discuss the physical features of the schools, the type or size of classes, the teaching styles of the instructors, or all of these. In the beginning of your paper, make it clear to the reader what you will discuss.
3. In one paragraph, agree with, disagree with, or explain the following quotation: "Education is one of the chief obstacles to intelligence and freedom of thought." —*Bertrand Russell*
4. Write a paragraph explaining what it takes to succeed in school. Consider the following to help you get started: intelligence, self-discipline, interest and motivation, supportive parents, financial support.
5. Write a paragraph about a teacher who had a strong influence on you. Describe how this teacher changed you and what he or she did to bring about the change. In your description, be specific about the teacher's attitude and/or behavior to give the reader a clear picture of this person.

free choice

6. Write a paragraph about any issue related to education that interests you.

PART four
Evaluating for Rewriting

Working with Your Partner

Exchange the paragraphs you wrote for the Writing Assignments section. Use the following questionnaire to evaluate each other's paragraphs.

1. Underline the topic sentence. Does it have all the characteristics for a good topic sentence discussed in Chapter One?

   Yes _____ No _____

2. Read the rest of the paragraph. Does each sentence relate to and develop the topic sentence?

   Yes _____ No _____

   If the answer is *no,* find the irrelevant sentences and underline them.

3. Put a star next to the explanatory (bridge) sentence, if there is one. Does it help you understand the main idea?

   Yes _____ No _____

   Why? Why not? ____

   ____

4. How many examples are there? List them briefly here:

   ____

   ____

   ____

   ____

   ____

5. Is there a restatement of the main idea in the last sentence?

   Yes _____ No _____

Rcturn each other's paragraphs. Read your partner's evaluation of your paragraph. Discuss any questions you have with your partner.

Working on Your Own

Now you are ready to evaluate your own paragraph. Consider you partner's evaluation comments. Do you need to rewrite your topic sentence? Do you need to add more information? Do you need to eliminate any irrelevant information? What other changes, if any, do you need to make?

Rewrite your paragraph, making any necessary changes. Turn this revised draft of your paragraph in to your teacher.

CHAPTER three

Relationships

in this chapter

You will interview an American about his or her family and write about the roles and relationships in your own family.

PART one
Ideas for Writing

Getting Started

A typical American family today is very different from a typical American family of forty years ago. The basic family structure has gone through many changes in the past few decades; however, particular relationships within families have always changed. As family members grow older, their roles—the functions and responsibilities they perform—change, and this often results in new relationships.

Look at the photos of some American families here and guess the relationships between the people in each picture. Share your guesses with a classmate and write them under each photo. The first one is done as an example.

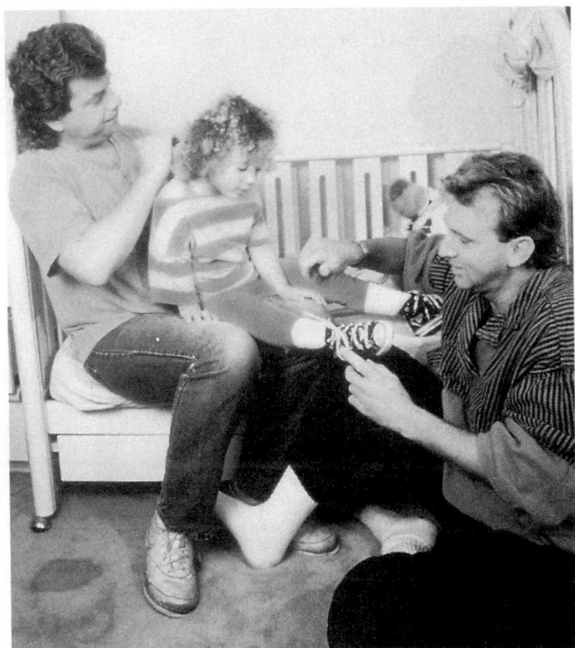

1. Four generations here—great grandmother and grandmother, mother and child

2. ______________________________

3. ______________________

4. ______________________

Brainstorming

The photos show changing families, or families in transition. Look again at the photos and write how these families may be changing.

1. ______________________
2. ______________________
3. ______________________
4. ______________________

Freewriting

Write for five minutes about some family changes that you have observed. You can write about American families or families from your own country.

Reading for Ideas

Kirsten is a student from Germany collecting information on the American family. Her assignment is to interview an American about his or her family to learn about the roles and relationships of family members. She is interviewing her neighbor, Audrey, a professional woman in her early forties. Before you read the interview, answer the following questions.

1. How are families in your country different today than they were forty years ago? What changes in roles have occurred? ______________________

____

____

2. How have relationships within your family changed over the years? Can you think of reasons for these changes? ______________________

____

____

An Interview with Audrey

KIRSTEN: Hi, Audrey! Thanks for helping me with this assignment.

AUDREY: Sure. What do you want to know?

KIRSTEN: Let's see . . . we're studying changes in families and changes in family relationships. I know you have grown children. Was your role as a parent like your mother's role when you were a child?

AUDREY: Oh, no! As parents, my mother and I were very different! Maybe this is because we are so different in other ways. We haven't always gotten along very well, but we had extremely different backgrounds. My mother came from a traditional Swedish family and was not educated beyond high school. My brothers and I were the first in her family to go

to college. The difference in our roles could also have been a result of the times—women were entering the work force, and men were helping out at home.

KIRSTEN: And you have always worked, haven't you?

AUDREY: Yes, I have either been teaching or going to school. My husband has been willing to share many of the household and parenting responsibilities with me, and the kids helped out as they were growing up. This was so different from my mother. Her husband, my dad, was a truckdriver and often away from home. So my mom stayed home and took care of us.

KIRSTEN: How did your children help out?

AUDREY: Well, we didn't have a dishwasher until just recently. The whole family cleaned up after dinner and washed and dried the dishes. The kids had to keep their rooms clean and do their own laundry.

KIRSTEN: And when you were a child, your mother did all that, right?

AUDREY: Yes. My mother also did all the cooking. It was very rare to meet a husband—or father—who cooked when I was young.

KIRSTEN: How about your husband? Does he cook?

AUDREY: Yes, he's quite a good cook. We often cook meals together, or he cooks by himself. Most of the time now, since the kids are out of the house, we go out to eat.

KIRSTEN: Do you see your children often?

AUDREY: We have family gatherings on major holidays where everyone—even my mother—gets together. My children are very independent and very different from each other, but we have always gotten along well.

KIRSTEN: So your relationship hasn't changed since your children have gotten older, but how about your roles? Do you notice a difference?

AUDREY: Yes, I think so. They sometimes take on the parenting role. For example, when the kids come home nowadays, they have lots of advice for us: get more exercise, eat healthy food, and take it easy. It's different to have them giving *us* advice.

KIRSTEN: And your mother? Does she still give you advice, or have your roles changed, too?

AUDREY: No, our roles haven't changed—my mother still has *lots* of advice for me. But now I just listen to her and say, "OK, Mom, you're right" instead of getting angry.

KIRSTEN: It sounds like you've changed too. Thanks for your time, Audrey. This has been really helpful.

AUDREY: You're welcome. If you need any more information, give me a call.

postreading questions

1. What facts do you remember about Audrey and her family from reading the interview?

   ____

   ____

2. Compare Audrey's role as a parent to her mother's role. What is similar and what is different? ____

   ____

   ____

3. Based on Audrey's family and your knowledge of other families, how have the roles of husbands, children, and grandparents changed since Audrey was a child? ____

   ____

   ____

4. Audrey describes her relationship with her mother as unchanged over the years. Do you think that the relationship between Audrey and her mother will ever change? Why or why not? To what extent is their relationship dependent on their roles, or on their perceptions of their roles?

5. What causes family relationships to change? Give some specific examples of changed relationships you have observed.

6. Are there any similarities between Audrey's family and your family?

THINKING CRITICALLY

Making Comparisons

You are going to develop a list of similarities and differences between Audrey's family life as a child and her family life as an adult. This is called *comparing*, and it is an important critical thinking skill.

1. **Decide what aspect of family life you want to compare, such as the mother's role, the father's role, relationships between family members, etc. Use Kirsten's questions for ideas. Make a chart for your comparison like the one below. In your chart, fill in the similarities and differences.**

Topic: The Mother's Role in the Family

When Audrey Was a Child	When Audrey Was a Parent
Her mother stayed home.	She had to work or go to school.

2. **Share your comparison with your classmates when you are finished.**

Gathering Information

Interview an American about his or her family. Ask about family roles, relationships, and feelings. Ask also about changes the family has faced and about past and present experiences. You will use this information as the basis for a writing assignment later in the chapter, so take notes. Use some of the questions Kirsten asked to get you started.

AN INTERVIEW WITH ______________________

Question 1: ______________________

____

____

Answer: ______________________

____

____

Question 2: ______________________

____

____

Answer: ______________________

____

____

Question 3: ______________________

____

____

Answer: ______________________

____

____

Question 4: ______________________

____

____

Answer: ______________________

____

____

Question 5: ____

____

____

Answer: ____

____

____

PART two
Language for Writing

Describing People: Roles and Relationships

The following chart contains expressions you can use to describe a person's **roles** and **relationships** within a family. Remember that one's role refers to the function he or she fulfills or duty he or she performs. (For example, Audrey's mother raised the children.) One's relationship to another person refers to a family tie (Bill is Audrey's brother; Sam is Audrey's son), or it refers to one's feelings about another person (whether a family member or not).

roles	relationships
Being the oldest, Megan *set an example* for her brother and sister.	Vivian *was close* to her sister Linda when they were young, but now they seldom see each other.
Danny *had more responsibilities* than his younger siblings; he had to wake everyone up, make the lunches and take the kids to school.	Kevin's parents *are more compatible* these days: They share housework and play golf together.
Audrey's father did not *play an active role* in raising his children because he was so busy with work.	Dara and her brother *don't get along* because of the great difference between them in age and interests.

Study the following additional expressions. Put a checkmark (✔) next to the expressions that describe a friend or family member you know.

	He *plays an important role* in his family.
	He *is an example* for his younger brother and sister.
	She *has a lot of responsibilities.*
	His parents *depend on* him for many things.
	They *are very compatible.*
	She *confides in* her mother.
	They *have a lot in common.*
	She *is close to* her aunt.
	The family *gets together* every weekend.
	She and her mother *don't get along.*
	He *is jealous* of his brother.
	Their parents never *favor* one of them; they *treat them equally.*
	He *shows respect* by listening carefully when his grandfather speaks.
	I don't like being *an only child* because I have no brothers or sisters to play with.

There are many other words that can help you describe roles and relationships in families. Review the word lists on the next page with a classmate and provide a synonym or explanation for each word. Add your own words to the lists.

NOUNS	VERBS	ADJECTIVES
sibling	share	competitive
relative	respect	related
relationship	misbehave	compatible
respect	favor	mature
stepmother,	punish	independent
stepfather	influence	respectful
cousin	quarrel	authoritative
great-grandparent	disagree	________
conflict	marry	________
twin	________	________
member	________	________
influence	________	________
________	________	________
________	________	________

Did you find any words that belong in more than one column?

Practicing What You've Learned

Choose the word or phrase that best expresses the meaning of the underlined words in the five sentences below.

1. She <u>is close to</u> her aunt.
- **a.** is similar in size to
- **b.** is the same age as
- **c.** has a deep and loving relationship with
- **d.** was named for

2. I don't like being <u>an only child</u>.
- **a.** home alone
- **b.** without brothers or sisters
- **c.** lonely
- **d.** the youngest

3. She and her mother <u>get along well</u>.
- **a.** have frequent disagreements
- **b.** go places together
- **c.** enjoy each other's company
- **d.** live close to each other

4. They <u>have a lot in common</u>.
- **a.** look alike
- **b.** are the same age
- **c.** share many interests
- **d.** own property

5. She <u>confides in</u> her mother.
- **a.** shares personal information with
- **b.** hides from
- **c.** has confidence in
- **d.** quarrels with

exercise 2 Write a paragraph about Audrey's family. Focus on the feelings she has about her mother, husband, and children. Use the vocabulary you've learned in this section.

exercise 3 Write a paragraph about your family. Choose either roles or relationships as the focus of your paragraph. Use the ideas from Freewriting in Part One to get started.

exercise 4 What special role does a father have in a family in your country? A mother? A grandfather? A grandmother? The oldest child? The middle child? The youngest child? Answer one of these questions in a paragraph.

exercise 5 What special role does a female have in a family from your country? A male? Write a paragraph in response to one of these questions.

PART three
Systems for Writing

From Paragraph to Essay

Review Points

- In a *unified* paragraph, all the sentences relate to and develop the topic sentence.
- In an *organized* paragraph, all the sentences are in a logical order.

In the previous chapters, you were explaining your ideas in paragraphs. Now you're going to learn how to expand a paragraph into an essay.

Read the following paragraph by Christine Vu, who is writing about the advantages of being the oldest daughter. Then answer the questions with a classmate.

When I was younger, I hated being the oldest child and the only girl in my family. But now that I am older, I realize that being "Big Sister" actually has its advantages. First of all, I get special treatment from my parents and brothers. I get my own room, and my brothers have to do all the heavy work around the house. Another benefit is that, being the oldest, I have learned to be responsible and dependable. For example, my parents often leave my brothers in my care when they go out. I also strive for the best in whatever I do in order to be a good role model for my brothers. The experience I've had taking care of my brothers has prepared me for my own family in the future. So, even though I didn't choose to be the oldest child and the only girl in my family, I have succeeded in making this situation work to my best advantage.

Christine Vu

1. What is the main idea of the paragraph?

____

____

____

2. What reasons does the writer give to support her main idea?

____

____

____

____

____

3. If you were to expand this paragraph into an essay, which points would you develop? Where could you provide more explanation?

____

____

____

____

The Essay

New Points

- In an essay, the writer states an opinion and supports that opinion.
- The writer can support her or his opinion by explaining, describing, comparing, defending or a combination of these.
- An academic essay is usually at least four paragraphs long.
- An academic essay includes an introduction, the main discussion (the *body*) and a conclusion.
- The main idea for the entire essay is called the *thesis statement*.

Now read how Christine has expanded her paragraph into an essay:

Advantages of Being the Oldest and Only Girl in the Family

When I was younger, I hated being the oldest child and only girl in my family. I can still remember telling my mom how I wished I was the youngest and had a sister instead. But, as I grew older, I realized that being the "Big Sister" wasn't so bad after all. Being the oldest and only girl has many advantages: I get special treatment from my family members, I have become a mature person, and I am better prepared for my own family in the future.

Although it is sometimes difficult, most of the time I enjoy being the oldest and only girl in the family. My parents and brothers treat me as though I'm a princess. For example, my brothers all have to follow my orders. If they do not, my parents will punish them. In addition, I get my own room with my own phone and television set and I don't have to share any of my clothes with anyone. My brothers, on the other hand, all have to share one room and wear hand-me-down clothes. Furthermore, I don't have to do any of the dirty or heavy work at home. Taking out the garbage, vacuuming the house, and washing the car are jobs for my brothers. As a little girl reading fairy tales long ago, I can remember always wanting to be the princess in the story; I never realized that in fact my family treated me like a princess.

Another benefit of being the oldest child is that I have developed many qualities that have made me a mature individual. Through experience, I have learned to be responsible and dependable, as well as earnest. For example, my parents go out on weekends and leave my brothers in my care; they believe that I can take care of and watch out for the safety of my brothers at home. By putting their trust in me, my parents have taught me to take responsibility. Besides my parents, my brothers also depend on me. They rely on me to help them with their schoolwork as well as with their problems in dealing with growing up. Again, since I want my brothers to know that they can depend on me, I have learned to be dependable. Not only did I learn to be responsible and dependable, I have also learned to be earnest. Since I'm a role model for my brothers, I strive for the best in whatever I do so that I will set a good example for them. That is, I have to do well in school and never give up on any task given to me no matter how difficult it may be. At first, I resented being the first-born in the family, but as I have become more mature, I have realized that it has really strengthened my character.

One other advantage of being the oldest daughter is that it has trained me to be ready for my own family in the future. In fact, in many ways I'm the mother figure at home. For instance, I cook dinner for my family and do most of the grocery shopping when my mom is not home or is too busy. When my dad's or brother's pants or shirts are torn, I mend them. When my brothers were younger, I used to take them to school and to the doctor in place of my parents. Even though having a family of my own in the future won't be easy, my experiences with my immediate family now will make it a much easier job for me later on.

Nobody said that life is easy; a person has to accept who he is and he must learn to live with and make the best of his situation. I didn't choose to be the oldest child and only girl in my family: I was born to be in this position. By realizing this fact, I have succeeded in making this situation work toward my best advantage. That is, I feel that my life is better because of this experience.

Christine Vu

Practicing What You've Learned

exercise 1 Complete the following outline of the essay you just read, "Advantages of Being the Oldest and Only Girl in the Family."

I. Introduction and thesis statement

____

____

____

II. First idea

____

____

____

III. Second idea

____

____

____

IV. Third Idea

____

____

____

V. Conclusion

____

____

____

exercise 2 Now compare the essay to Christine Vu's original paragraph on page 61 and answer these questions.

1. What parts of the essay are the same as or similar to the paragraph?

____

____

____

2. What parts of the essay are new?

____

____

____

3. Where were these new parts added?

____

____

____

4. Can you identify any of these new parts as: (a) supporting ideas, (b) explanations, (c) illustrations, (d) examples?

____

____

____

5. Why were the new parts added?

____

____

____

Look at the following diagram, which shows how the parts of the paragraph relate to those of the essay:

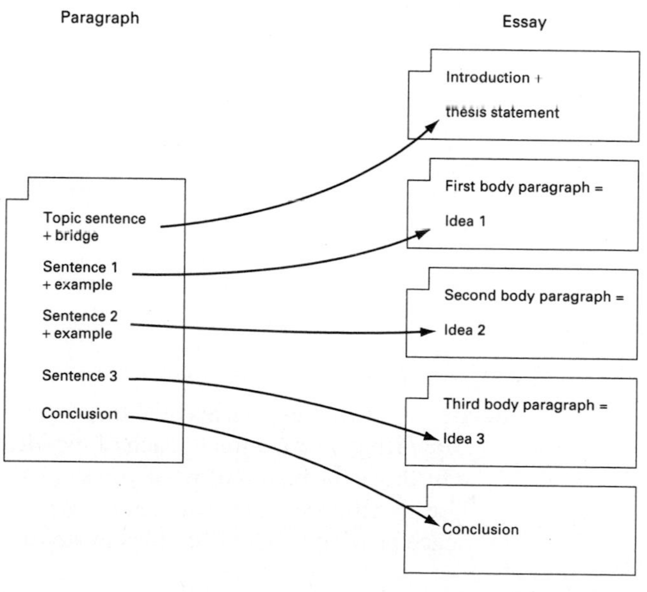

Expand this paragraph into an essay by completing the three steps that follow.

My parents played an important role in my educational development by helping me in both material and spiritual ways to become the person that I am today. They raised my older brothers and sisters in such a way that they would set a good example for me and the other younger children. They bought various books that helped me become a hard-working student and a good reader. They also exposed me to experiences such as vacations and museum trips that enlarged my perspective on life. In addition, they looked carefully at my examination results in school in order to motivate me always to do my best. In short, I owe all of my positive qualities to the efforts of my parents. —*Solomon Gebreaftse*

1. Make an outline in note form of the paragraph.

Write the topic sentence here: ____________________

____

____

____

What is idea 1? ____________________

____

____

____

What is idea 2? ____________________

____

____

____

What is idea 3? ____________________

____

____

____

What is idea 4? ____________________

____

____

____

2. Based on your experience and the reading you've done in this chapter, add supporting information to each of the ideas in step 1. You can do this by giving a further explanation of what you think the writer means by each of his ideas. Use specific examples and details. Write your supporting points in the extra space provided under each idea in step 1.

3. Now write an essay based on your outline. Remember that the paragraphs, although part of an essay, should contain all the elements you've been practicing in the book up to this point.

Here is another paragraph that you can expand into a complete essay by further developing the main ideas. Notice that while this paragraph is on a topic similar to Christine Vu's on pages 62 and 63, the author mentions both the positive and negative sides of being the oldest daughter. First, read the paragraph.

The responsibility of taking care of a home can be a great burden to the oldest daughter in a family, especially if she is still in school. However, this responsibility also gives her the opportunity to gain experience that will later help her in her marriage or college life. The disadvantage of being the oldest daughter is that when she becomes responsible for doing all of the housework, she may have a difficult time keeping up with her studies, since both take a considerable amount of time and energy. There is, however, at least one advantage to being the oldest daughter in the family. If she has previously experienced the "housewife role" while growing up, she may be able to avoid the trial-and-error approach many women have to go through when they first get married and have children. Even if the oldest daughter does not choose to get married, her knowledge and experience in taking care of a house will be helpful once she leaves home to live on her own. Thus, being the oldest daughter has both advantages and disadvantages.

Stephanie J. Kim

Now, follow steps 1 through 3 from Exercise 3. Try to use information that is different from Christine Vu's essay. Note that there are only *two* ideas to expand in Stephanie Kim's paragraph. How many paragraphs will this essay have?

Write a paragraph on one of these topics concerning family roles and relationships.

1. Roles in the family (parents, oldest, youngest, boy, girl)
2. Relationships with siblings
3. Parents' responsibilities
4. Parents' relationship with each other
5. Changes in the family over time
6. Families across cultures

Make an outline like the ones in Exercises 3 and 4. Then expand your paragraph into an essay. Share your original paragraph, the outline, and the essay with a classmate before you give it to your teacher.

Expand one of the paragraphs you wrote in a previous chapter into a four- or five-paragraph essay. First, make an outline. Give the original paragraph, the outline, and the new essay to your teacher.

focus on testing

Making an Outline

Exercises 3, 4, 5, and 6 ask you to make an outline before you write your essay. Whenever you write an essay under time pressure, list the main ideas in outline form and develop your supporting ideas from the outline. This will help you save time and keep your writing focused.

Writing Assignments

Write an essay on one of the following topics. Use new vocabulary and expressions you learned in this chapter and make sure that your paragraphs are clear and coherent. Develop your ideas by using information from the research you did in Part One.

1. Write an essay about the advantages and/or disadvantages of your position in your family (that is, on being the oldest, youngest, middle, or only child).
2. Write an essay in which you describe your relationship with your brothers and sisters.
3. Write an essay in which you describe your parents' relationship with each other.
4. Write an essay in which you explain how your parents' relationship with each other affected you and/or your brothers and sisters as you were growing up.
5. Write an essay describing how roles and relationships in your family have changed over the years.
6. Write an essay based on the interview you did in Part One. Use one of the topics of Assignments 1–5 above.
7. Write an essay in which you compare one aspect of family life in your culture and in North American culture. For example, you may choose to discuss the role of the father in raising children, the role of grandparents, the responsibility of male or female children, loyalty to the family, or how couples meet.
8. Write an essay including facts about the typical family in your home country or city today. Focus on roles or relationships (or both).
9. Expand a paragraph you've already written to a four- to five-paragraph essay.

free choice

10. Write an essay on any aspect of relationships that interests you.

PART four
Evaluating for Rewriting

Working with Your Partner

step 1

Exchange the essays you wrote for the Writing Assignments section. Use the following questionnaire to evaluate each other's essays.

1. How many paragraphs does the essay have? _____

2. Locate each part of the essay; indicate which paragraph it corresponds to:

Introduction	Paragraph number _____
Body	Paragraph number _____
	Paragraph number _____
	Paragraph number _____
Conclusion	Paragraph number _____

Do any parts in the essay not correspond to one of the essay parts above?

Yes _____ No _____

If the answer is *yes,* consider whether to eliminate this part or incorporate it into another part of the essay.

3. Is there a thesis statement (a sentence that tells you what the entire essay is to be about)? If so, underline it. Does it *really* prepare you for the essay that follows?

Yes _____ No _____

If the answer is *no,* how could your partner improve the thesis statement?

4. Put an **X** next to the topic sentences of each body paragraph. Does each topic sentence tell the reader what the paragraph is about?

Yes _____ No _____

If the answer is *no* for any of the topic sentences, how could your partner improve it?

5. Do the ideas in each of the body paragraphs relate to the topic sentence?

Yes _____ No _____

Put a **?** next to each sentence that does not develop the topic sentence so your partner can revise them.

Return each other's essays. Read your partner's evaluation of your essay. Discuss any questions you have with your partner.

Working on Your Own

Now you should be ready to evaluate your own essay. Go through the questions again, keeping in mind what your partner said about your essay when he or she evaluated it. Pay particular attention to the form. Does it have all the necessary parts? Is there a statement that tells the reader what the essay is about?

Rewrite your essay, making any necessary changes. Turn this revised draft of your essay in to your teacher.

CHAPTER four

Health

in this chapter

You will interview people about the importance of health in their lives and write about the causes and effects of good health.

PART one
Ideas for Writing

Getting Started

Many things affect a person's health: diet, work, weather, leisure-time activities, and mental attitude. This chapter explores issues in health and how they affect people in both positive and negative ways. How is your health affected by your diet? Your work? The weather? Your hobbies? Your attitudes and moods? Discuss the answers to these questions with a classmate.

Look closely at the photos here and on the next page and answer the questions that follow.

1. What health problems do you think the woman in photo 1 might have? Why? ______________________

____

____

1.

2.

2. What are the women in photo 2 going to eat? How will their choices affect their health? ______________________

____

____

3.

4.

3. Why are the commuters in photo 3 upset? How does a hurried lifestyle affect one's health? ____________________

____

____

4. Describe the commuter in photo 4. ____________________

____

____

5. In what ways does the type of work a person does affect his or her physical and mental well-being? Give additional examples of jobs that have positive or negative effects on health. ____________________

____

____

5.

6.

Now, discuss *your* lifestyle choices: How do you get to school each day? What kind of food do you eat? How does your work affect your health? What else do you do that has positive or negative effects on your health?

Brainstorming

Look at the photos again, and, in small groups, talk about the causes of good health and poor health. Discuss physical and mental health and go as deeply into the topic as possible. As you talk, keep notes in the following chart on the words and expressions that you use.

	CAUSE(S) →	EFFECT
1.	eats too much junk food, doesn't exercise	overweight
2.	________________________	__________
3.	________________________	__________
4.	________________________	__________
5.	________________________	__________
6.	________________________	__________

Freewriting

Choose one of the pictures at the beginning of the chapter and write for seven minutes without stopping. Write about what the person is doing, why she or he is doing it, and how you think she or he is feeling mentally and/or physically.

Reading for Ideas

You are going to read an article from the *New York Times* about health and personality. Before you read, do the following activity.

prereading questions

What kind of person are you? Take this quiz and discuss your answers with the class.

1. You are in the express checkout line at the supermarket, where there is a limit of ten items. The person in front of you has more than ten items.
   a. How do you feel? ____________________
   b. What do you do? ____________________
2. You are trying to park your car in the busy downtown area of a big city. You finally see a good parking place and signal that you are going to back into it. Suddenly, a car behind you pulls into the spot without any warning.
   a. How do you feel? ____________________
   b. What do you do? ____________________
3. Do you think most people are basically honest? ____________________
4. Do you frequently yell at people who make you angry? ____________________
5. Would you describe yourself as *cynical?* (Look this up if you are not sure of the meaning.) ____________________
6. Have you ever hit someone because you were angry? ____________________
7. When something makes you angry, how long do you *stay* angry? ____________________
8. Do you feel that you have a lot of hassles, or disputes, in your everyday life? ____________________

Cynicism and Mistrust Tied to Early Death

A psychiatrist has found that people who are angry and cynical are five times as likely to die under the age of 50 as people who are calm and trusting. This differs from what many researchers used to believe: that Type A people—people who work too hard and are always in a hurry—were likely to die early from heart disease. The psychiatrist Dr. Redford B. Williams believes that his work disproves the Type A theory. He feels that hostility, rather than stress, leads to premature death.

During the 1970s, Dr. Meyer Friedman and Dr. Ray Rosenman, cardiologists in San Francisco, identified "Type A" men. Type A men, according to the cardiologists, were twice as likely to suffer heart disease as relaxed men, a group they labeled "Type B." However, a series of studies conducted in the early 1980s failed to prove that there was a connection between Type A personalities and heart problems.

"We can now state with some confidence that of all the aspects that make up the Type A pattern, only those related to hostility and anger really lead to heart problems," Williams said.

Williams based his findings on numerous studies, including a 25-year study of 118 lawyers. The study participants took a standard personality test when they were in law school. Those who received high scores on hostility traits were five times as likely to die before age 50 as classmates who were not hostile. Personality traits such as paranoia ("People are picking on me"), social avoidance ("I'd rather cross the street than meet that person"), and neurotic behaviors were not related to early death. However, personality traits that reflected cynical mis-

postreading questions

1. According to the article, what kind of personality type is likely to die young?

___

___

2. What kind of health problems do angry, cynical people tend to have?

___

___

3. Describe a Type A personality. Is this kind of person likely to have heart disease? Explain.

___

___

___

___

trust ("People lie to get ahead"), anger, and angry behavior ("I often have to get rough with people") were strong predictors of premature death.

Cynicism and anger are expressed in everyday events, Williams said. For example, many people get annoyed or anxious when, in an express checkout line at the grocery store, other people have more than the allowed number of items. The angry personality type will not just feel upset, Williams said. He will act on his anger. Furthermore, angry people report more problems in their everyday lives, he said.

Hostile and nonhostile people seem to have fundamentally different nervous systems, Williams said. When nonhostile people become upset, their nervous system acts like a "stop switch" that calms them down. Hostile people, on the other hand, seem to have weak nervous systems—they can't calm down. The levels of adrenaline in their bodies remain high, and they stay unpleasantly aroused and continue to feel angry, Williams said.

These differences appear in infancy. When they become upset, hostile people also have larger rises in blood pressure than nonhostile people. This can lead to damage of the heart and blood vessels in hostile people. The hearts of calm, trusting people last longer, Williams claimed, because they are protected from the damage the nervous system can cause.

"I think we should abandon the Type A hypothesis," Williams stated. "There is no evidence that the Type A personality is likely to die young. But there is lots of evidence that people who are hostile and angry do."

Sandra Blakeslee

4. Explain how an angry, cynical person might react to situations 1 and 2 in the prereading exercise on page 75.

____

____

____

5. Explain in your own words the differences between what happens when a hostile person gets upset and when a nonhostile person gets upset.

____

____

____

6. In your opinion, is it possible for a person to change his or her basic personality characteristics?

____

____

THINKING CRITICALLY

Analyzing Sources

Work in small groups and analyze the information on the study of lawyers in paragraph 4 of "Cynicism and Mistrust Tied to Early Death." What is your opinion of the study? Was it a valid basis for William's conclusions? Are there enough details about the study to convince you of William's conclusions? *Analyzing* the source of a scientific finding is a useful critical thinking skill.

The following questions might help you analyze the study:

- **What was the gender of the lawyers in the study? Is this important?**
- **Why were only lawyers chosen to participate in the study? Does it make any difference that all survey participants had the same profession?**

You and your classmates may or may not decide that the study and/or the information that the reporter chose to include about it was adequate. Either way, it's a good idea to consider *how* researchers arrive at their conclusions when you read scientific material.

Gathering Information

Find out to what extent the average American is concerned about his or her health. Interview at least five Americans using the chart on the facing page. You can add your own questions at the bottom of the chart.

	person 1	person 2	person 3	person 4	person 5
1. On a scale of 1 to 5, with 5 being most important, how important is health in your day-to-day life?	1 2 3 4 5	1 2 3 4 5	1 2 3 4 5	1 2 3 4 5	1 2 3 4 5
2. What are three things you do every day to stay healthy?	______ ______ ______	______ ______ ______	______ ______ ______	______ ______ ______	______ ______ ______
3. Think of three life goals. Rank them in order of importance. (*Examples:* financial independence, a successful career, a home, a happy marriage, having children, etc.) 1st: 2nd: 3rd:	______ ______ ______	______ ______ ______	______ ______ ______	______ ______ ______	______ ______ ______
4. Where do you rank health in comparison with your three life goals? (1st, 2nd, 3rd, 4th, etc.)	______	______	______	______	______
5. Your own questions:					

Language for Writing

Showing Causes and Effects

Causes and effects often enter into discussions of health. The following list contains expressions for discussing causes and effects.

One (The) cause of + *noun* is + *noun.*

Noun { leads to / results in / results from / causes / has an effect on } + *noun.*

As a result of + *noun,* . . .
As a result, + *sentence*

Because / Since } + *clause,* . . .
Because of + *noun,* . . .

The (One) effect (result) of + *noun* is that. . . .

Examples: One cause of poor health is a lack of exercise.

Layla doesn't exercise much.

As a result, she is suffering from poor health.

A lack of exercise can lead to poor health.

Smoking causes lung cancer.

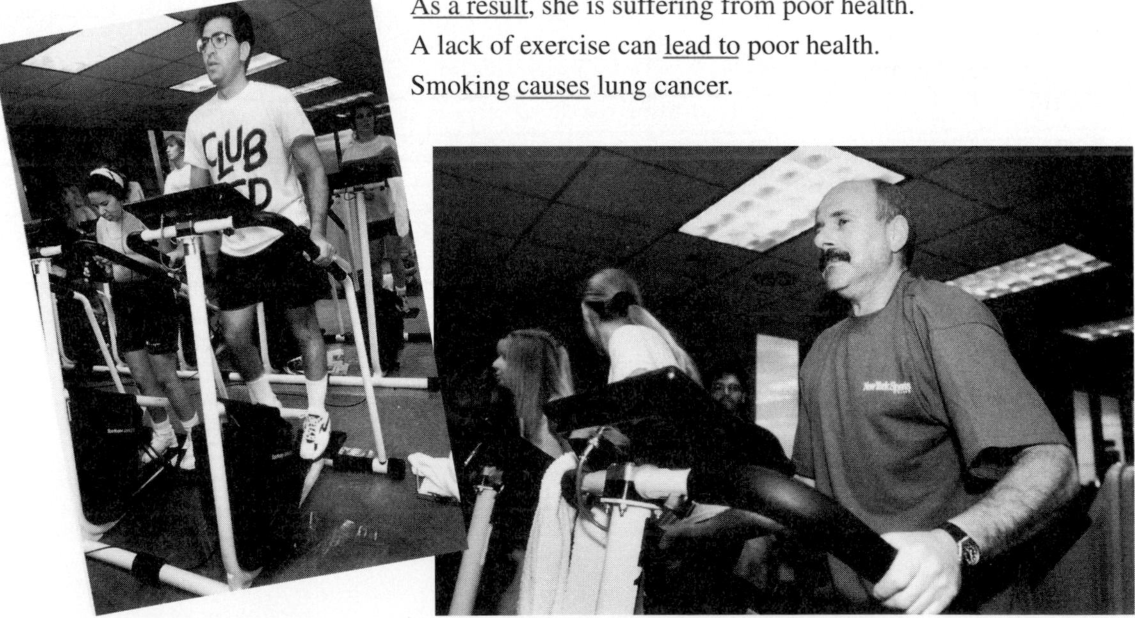

Describing Influences on Health

Here are some words and expressions that are useful in describing things that influence a person's health.

NOUNS	VERBS	ADJECTIVES
attitude	change	hurried
risk	risk	angry
money	increase	happy
social life	control	relaxed
friends	choose	tense
stress	enjoy	stressful
diet	suffer (from)	ambitious
work		competitive
lifestyle		active
pressure		well-balanced
family		
environment		

Practicing What You've Learned

Look at the following chart. On the right are some common health conditions, and on the left are causes for these conditions. Match each health condition with its appropriate cause. Some conditions may have more than one cause. Note that some of the nouns in the Effects column are uncountable.

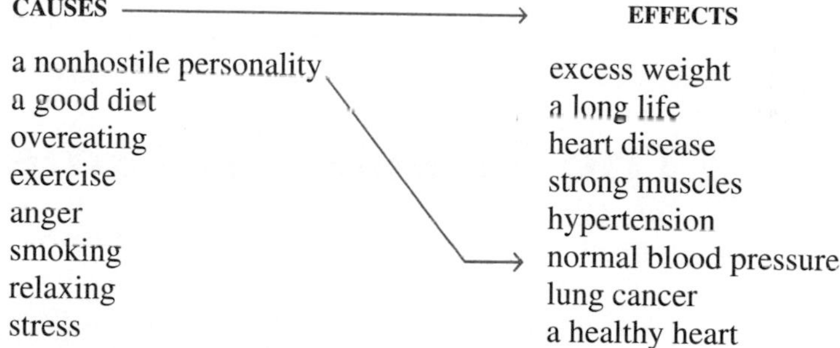

CAUSES →	EFFECTS
a nonhostile personality	excess weight
a good diet	a long life
overeating	heart disease
exercise	strong muscles
anger	hypertension
smoking	normal blood pressure
relaxing	lung cancer
stress	a healthy heart

After you match the causes and the effects, use each one in a sentence with the cause and effect expressions on page 80.

example: *A good diet results in a long life.*

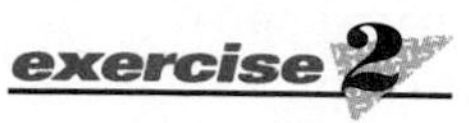

Write one sentence for each of the photos in Part One. Describe how the actions of the people in the photos probably affect their health. Use words and expressions from this section.

Write a paragraph about your lifestyle. Describe how it affects your health. Use words and expressions from this section.

Read the following paragraph about high blood pressure. Find and underline any cause and effect expressions. Then rewrite the paragraph, replacing each cause and effect expression with a new one from the list at the beginning of this section.

High blood pressure places a severe strain on the heart, blood vessels, and kidneys. That strain may eventually cause the heart to enlarge and become thickened. In some cases, the heart may fail. High blood pressure can also cause the blood vessels to "overstretch," weaken, or burst; a ruptured blood vessel in the brain can cause a stroke or even paralysis. The third and most serious complication related to high blood pressure is kidney failure. When the kidneys cease to function, they no longer filter out waste products. The result of kidney failure may be serious illness, or even death.

PART three
Systems for Writing

Review Points

- An academic essay includes an introduction with a thesis statement, the main discussion, and a conclusion.
- An academic essay usually has four or more paragraphs.

The Thesis Statement

New Points

- A thesis statement expresses the main idea of an essay.
- It announces the topic and suggests the ways in which the writer will support her or his point of view.
- One way to write a thesis statement is to answer one or more information questions (*who, what, why*, in *what* way, *how*, and so forth).
- A thesis statement usually appears somewhere in the first paragraph of an essay. To start with, put it at the *end* of the first paragraph of your essay.

The following is a thesis statement from a five-paragraph essay about how lifestyle affects a person's health. Study the thesis statement and answer the questions.

> A positive mental attitude, regular exercise, and a well-balanced diet are all aspects of a lifestyle that can lead to good health.

1. Find the part of the thesis statement that expresses the topic of the essay and underline it.
2. Find the ideas in the thesis that support the topic. How many are there? Write them here.

____

____

____

____

____

____

____

3. Suppose that this thesis statement is the answer to a question. From the following list, choose the question that the thesis statement is an answer to:

_____ Does a person's lifestyle affect his or her health?

_____ What contributes to good health?

_____ How does a well-balanced diet result in good health?

4. Based on your understanding of this thesis statement, what do you think the essay it comes from is about?

____

____

____

____

____

____

5. Explain why the following is not a good thesis statement:

> Three aspects of a person's lifestyle can lead to good health.

As you probably noticed, this thesis statement is missing an important part: the supporting ideas.

focus on testing

Answering the Question

Whenever you have to write an essay that answers a question on a standardized test, follow these steps:

- Read the question carefully, and make sure you understand it.
- Write a thesis statement that answers the question.
- Then use the thesis statement as the basis for your essay.

Supporting Ideas

New Points

- Mention in your thesis only what you can realistically cover in your essay. You should be able to develop each supporting idea in one paragraph.
- Each supporting idea should have the same degree of generality; that is, don't mix a general idea with a very specific one. These supporting ideas have the same degree of generality:

  The Hunzukuts' longevity is due to heredity and lifestyle.

  These don't:

  The Hunzukuts' longevity is due to *heredity* and the fact that *they don't smoke.*

  This thesis is out of balance because *heredity* is a general idea and *not smoking* is a comparatively specific one.

Practicing What You've Learned

Read the following thesis statements and decide which are inadequate, according to the preceding guidelines about thesis statements. For each inadequate thesis statement, explain *why* it is inadequate and rewrite it to make it better. Work with one or two partners.

1. Higher education is a waste of time.
2. There are three main differences between U.S. culture and Japanese culture.
3. Research has shown that people will live longer if they avoid stress and don't eat sugar.
4. Smaller university classes are better than large ones because students get more individual attention and they have more opportunities to participate in class.

Students often have to write essays to answer questions on exams. Exams give students only a limited amount of time to write their essays. Therefore, being able to think quickly of a thesis statement in response to a question is a useful skill. To practice this skill, read the questions here and on the next page and write a thesis statement in response to each one. Work quickly, as you would in a real test situation.

1. Should science and technology students have to take communication skills courses in college? ______________________________

____

____

____

2. What are the major differences between your culture and American culture? ______________________________

____

____

____

____

____

3. Should fathers assume as much responsibility in raising their children as mothers do? ______________________________

____

____

____

4. What is success?

5. What are the main causes of poor health among college students?

6. What are the advantages and disadvantages of living in a dormitory while in college?

7. Do the positive effects of advanced technology outweigh the negative effects?

8. How does environment affect mental health?

9. What can a college student learn about life *outside* of the classroom?

10. What are some of the effects of living in a crowded urban area?

When you finish, exchange your thesis statements with a partner and check each other's work. Make suggestions for improvement if necessary.

In this exercise, you are going to practice developing thesis statements.

1. Form small groups or work with the entire class. Have one student take notes. Your teacher will assign an essay topic from the Writing Assignments section below. Read it carefully to be sure you understand it.
2. Say everything and anything that comes into your mind about this topic. (The student taking notes will write all this down.) Don't be shy and don't hold anything back—even if you think it's silly or off the topic. Brainstorm like this for fifteen to twenty minutes.
3. Examine the ideas in your list. Do you detect a pattern? Is there one main idea that seems more significant than any other? Pick out the most important idea in the list. Could this be your point of view on the essay topic? If so, underline it twice.
4. Look in your list for two to three other ideas that relate to and support your point of view. Does each idea have the same degree of generality? Can you discuss each idea in one paragraph? Does each idea answer an information question about your point of view? If you answered yes to these questions, circle these supporting ideas.
5. Combine your point of view and your supporting ideas into one complete, clear statement. Now you have a thesis statement.
6. Evaluate your thesis according to the New Points presented on page 82. (If you've been working in groups, give your thesis to another group.) If it is approved, you're ready to write your essay. (Write your essay on your own, not as a group.)

Don't throw your notes away! They're valuable for developing your supporting ideas. Pick out specific details that relate to each of your supporting ideas. Make sure the details are relevant, concrete, and clear. See how easy it is to get started on a writing assignment? You may even have found that the brainstorming process helped develop your point of view on the topic.

Writing Assignments

Write an essay on one of the following topics. Use new vocabulary and expressions you learned in this chapter; be sure your paragraphs are clear and coherent. Develop your ideas by using information from the research you did in Part One.

1. Write about causes and effects of good health. Use the interviews you conducted in Part One to support your topic sentence.
2. Write about the causes and effects of poor health. Again, use your interviews for support.
3. Argue for or against a particular remedy for an illness or health condition. Develop support for your argument by explaining what your remedy does or does not cause.
4. Discuss advantages or disadvantages of a particular health care system.
5. Agree/disagree with the proverb: "An apple a day keeps the doctor away."

6. Write an essay about any issue related to health that interests you.

Evaluating for Rewriting

Working with Your Partner

step 1

Exchange the essays you wrote for the Writing Assignments section. Use the following questionnaire to evaluate each other's essays.

1. Read only the first paragraph of the essay. Locate the thesis statement and write it in the following space.

   Thesis statement: ______________________________

   ____

   ____

2. Does it express the topic? Underline it twice. Are there supporting ideas? Circle them.

3. Look at the supporting ideas again. Write them here, and answer the following questions.

   Supporting idea 1: ______________________________

   ____

   Supporting idea 2: ______________________________

   ____

   Supporting idea 3: ______________________________

   ____

   a. Do each of the supporting ideas answer an information question about the topic? What are the information questions?

   1. ______________________________

      ____

   2. ______________________________

      ____

   3. ______________________________

      ____

b. Do you think a writer could develop each of the supporting ideas in one paragraph?

Yes _____ No _____

If the answer is *no,* make suggestions for revision.

____

____

____

____

c. Do all the supporting ideas have the same degree of generality?

Yes _____ No _____

If the answer is *no,* make suggestions for revision.

____

____

____

____

4. Describe in a couple of sentences what you think the essay is about, based on the thesis sentence. (Don't read the rest of the essay yet!)

____

____

____

____

5. Now read the rest of the essay. Was your description in question 4 correct?

Yes _____ No _____

If the answer is *no,* explain why the thesis statement did not prepare you for the essay and make suggestions for revision.

____

____

step 2

Return each other's essays. Read your partner's evaluation of your essay. Discuss any questions you have with your partner.

Working on Your Own

Now you should be ready to evaluate your own essay. Go through the questions again. Take into consideration what your partner said about your thesis statement when he or she evaluated it. Does it adequately prepare the reader for what is to follow? Is it clear? Is anything missing?

Rewrite your essay, making any necessary changes. Turn this revised draft of your essay in to your teacher.

CHAPTER five

High Tech, Low Tech

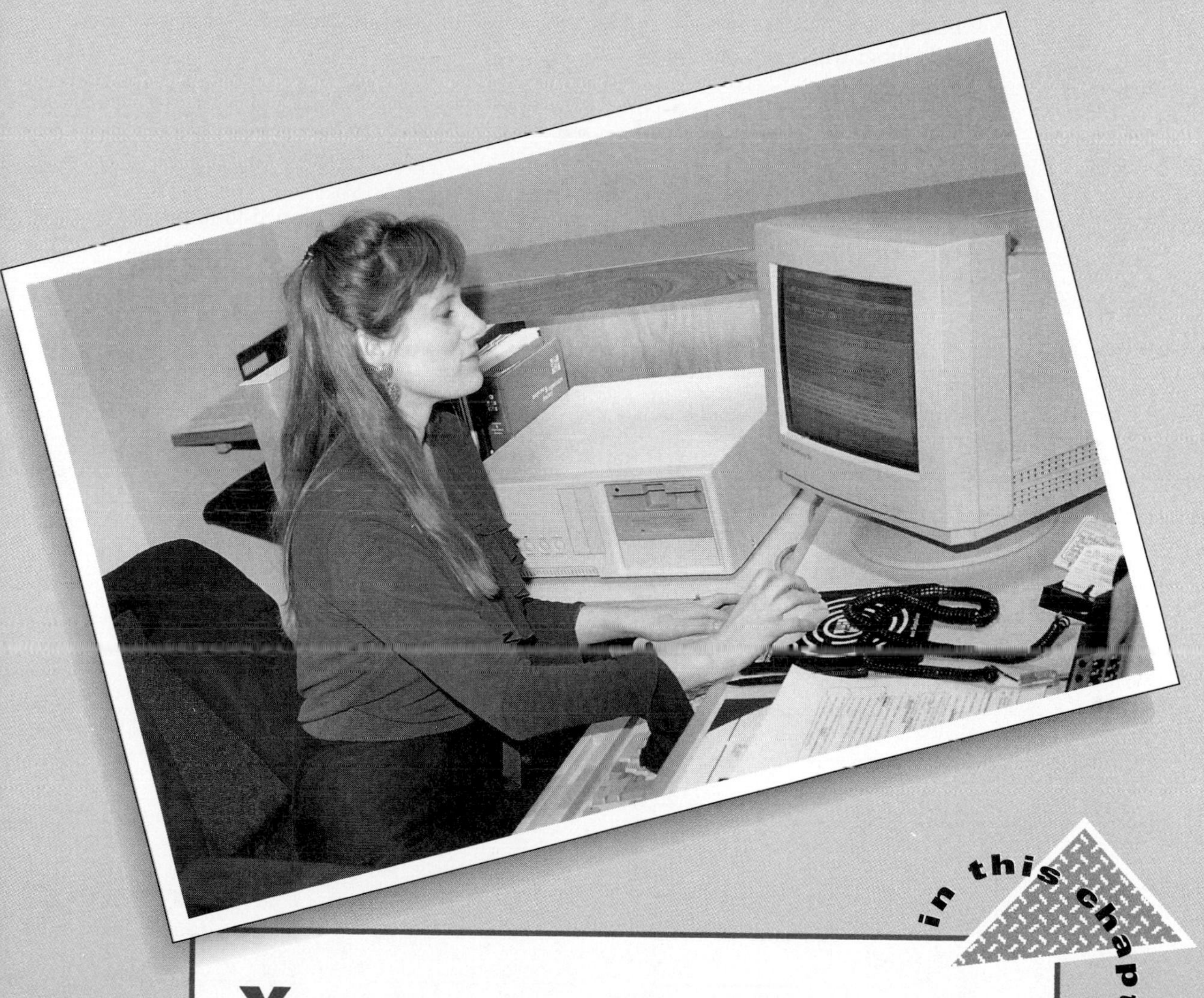

in this chapter

You will research a technological innovation and write about advances in technology.

PART one
Ideas for Writing

Getting Started

How have you come to depend on technology? In this chapter, you're going to think about the role technology plays in your life and its advantages and disadvantages.

With a classmate, discuss some of the ways you use technology on a regular basis. Then look at the photos of technological innovations on the facing page and talk about what each one shows.

Brainstorming

The photos show examples of technology that have been developed to improve different aspects of life. But sometimes such developments come with disadvantages. For each photo, list the way or ways this technological innovation makes life better. Then add any disadvantages you can think of. Some technological innovations may not have disadvantages. Add more examples of current technological innovations if you can. The first one is done as an example.

INNOVATION	ADVANTAGES	DISADVANTAGES
Robotics	Gets boring or dangerous work done faster. Creates technical and engineering jobs.	Eliminates certain kinds of jobs.

1. Robotic automobile assembly

2. Genetic engineering of crop plants

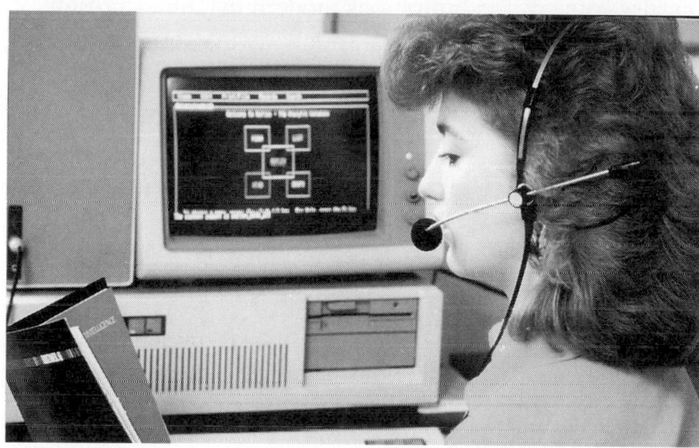

3. Operator with headset at voice-recognition computer

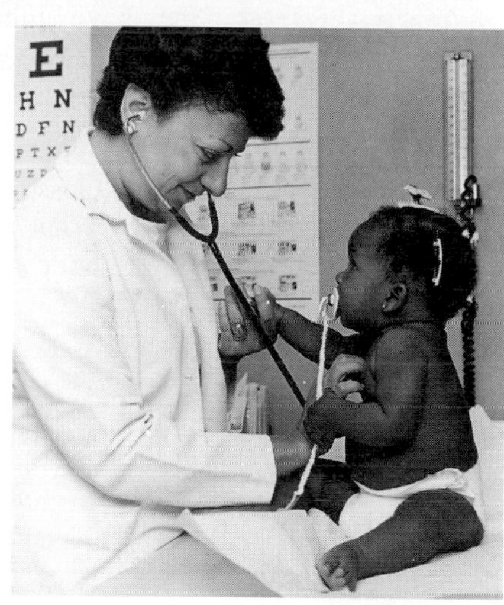

4. Micromachines for medical diagnosis

5. Communicating en route

6. Multimedia in education

Freewriting

Some people believe that through technology the world has become a safer and more comfortable place. Others believe that technology has taken people away from their natural environment and is dehumanizing. How do *you* feel about technology? Do the advantages outweigh the disadvantages?

Write for ten minutes about the advantages and/or disadvantages of technology. You can write about technology in general or about a specific technological innovation if you prefer.

Reading for Ideas

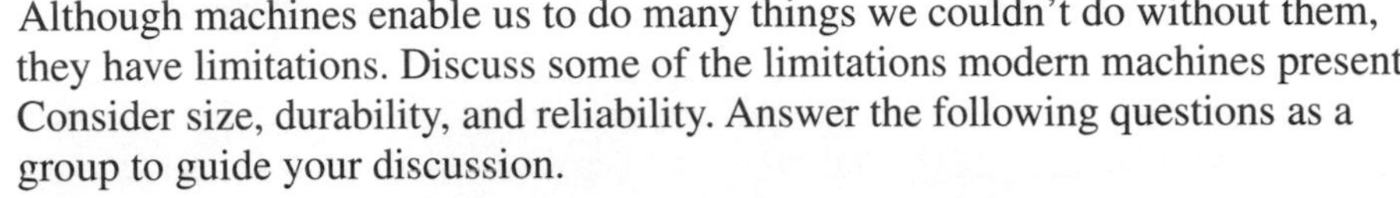

Although machines enable us to do many things we couldn't do without them, they have limitations. Discuss some of the limitations modern machines present. Consider size, durability, and reliability. Answer the following questions as a group to guide your discussion.

1. What are some things machines enable us to do? Make a list with your class.
2. What are some things we someday hope to do with the help of machines, but can't do yet?
3. What is a silicon chip? What kinds of machines use them?
4. What does *micro* mean? List some words with this prefix.

Now read the following magazine article, which describes a breakthrough in technology. This was written by Samuel Greengard, who writes about technological issues.

Small World

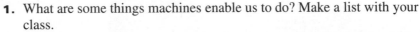

In the past, one of the biggest disadvantages of machines has been their inability to work on a micro- (or tiny) scale. For example, doctors did not have devices allowing them to go inside the human body to identify health problems or to perform delicate surgery. Repair crews did not have a way of identifying broken pipes located deep within a high-rise apartment building. However, that's about to change. Advances in computers and biophysics have started a microminiature revolution that's allowing scientists to envision—and in some cases actually build—microscopic machines. These devices promise to radically change the way we live and work.

Micromachines—sometimes referred to as nanotechnology—already are making an impact. At Case Western Reserve University in Cleveland, Ohio, research scientists have designed a 4-inch silicon chip that holds 700 tiny primitive motors. At Lucas NovaSensor in Fremont, California, scientists have perfected the world's first microscopic blood-pressure sensor. Threaded through a person's arteries, the sensor can provide blood pressure readings at the valve of the heart itself.

Micromachines have captured the interest of a wide range of industries. Automobile manufacturers soon will begin using tiny devices that run on static electricity to sense when to release an airbag and how to keep engines and brakes operating efficiently. Machines like these are likely to appear in airplanes and even space vehicles by the beginning of the next century. Some futurists envision nanotechnology also being used to explore the deep sea in small submarines, or even to launch finger-sized rockets packed with microminiature instruments.

A postage stamp and three sizes of blood pressure sensors.

The applications are most promising in the medical field. Cardiovascular Imaging Systems in Sunnyvale, California, manufactures a probe smaller than 1 millimeter that can provide snapshots of a patient's arteries. It's currently used in more than 200 cardiology centers around the world. Says Director of Marketing Adam Dakin: "Everybody is trying to create miniaturized devices for invasive surgery. There's no question that it will play a prominent role in the future."

Although simple versions of miniature devices have already had an impact, advanced versions and widespread use are still several years away. In Japan, scientists are designing an "intelligent" microdevice that can travel through the human digestive tract. And airplanes eventually might be able to twist and adapt their wings to be more efficient and flexible. Artificial body parts might provide total flexibility and full capabilities for people who have lost their natural limbs.

"There is an explosion of new ideas and applications," says Kurt Petersen, who eight years ago co-founded Lucas NovaSensor. So, when scientists now think about future machines doing large and complex tasks, they're thinking smaller than ever before.

Samuel Greengard

postreading questions

1. Over the years, many technological innovations have enabled us to perform tasks that are too large or heavy for human strength. How are the machines described in the article different? ______________________________

____

____

2. How big is a microminiature blood-pressure sensor? Show its size by comparing it to an object you have with you, or show its size by drawing it.

____

____

3. The author lists the size of micromachines as their biggest advantage. Are there other advantages to the "microminiature revolution" that the writer doesn't mention? Can you think of any disadvantages to micromachines?

____

____

4. Name some industries or fields that will benefit from micromachines. Can you think of additional fields the author doesn't mention?______________

____

____

5. Think about the tasks or operations micromachines can do now and the tasks or operations micromachines will be able to do in the future. With a classmate, list them below.

NOW	THE FUTURE
____________________	____________________
____________________	____________________
____________________	____________________
____________________	____________________

6. What does it mean to "think big?" In the conclusion, the writer says that scientists are thinking smaller. Is this good?____________________

____

____

Gathering Information

Research a technological innovation that interests you. First, locate the *Reader's Guide to Periodicals* in the library. Choose a topic and look for information about it in a recent copy of a magazine. Then make a list of what your innovation can and will be able to do, like the chart you have completed in the Postreading

Questions section. If you don't have access to the *Reader's Guide,* read something in your own language. Use the following list of topics to get you started. (The words in parentheses are subject headings you can look under in the *Reader's Guide*.)

1. Using computers as teaching machines (technology, computers, computer-assisted instruction, education)
2. Robots as workers (robotics, technology)
3. Eliminating congenital diseases through genetic engineering (genetic engineering)
4. Generating electricity through nuclear power (nuclear power)
5. Investigating life in space or on another planet (space exploration)
6. Arresting the growth of cancer cells through radiation therapy (radiation therapy)

THINKING CRITICALLY

Analyzing Pros and Cons

The advantages of a situation are called the *pros*. The disadvantages are called the *cons*. Considering the pros and cons of an issue helps you develop objectivity and is an important critical thinking skill.

Think about a technological innovation that is not widely available yet but that people are looking forward to using. Consider the pros and cons of this innovation. Work with one or two classmates, and present your results to the rest of the class. Use a format like this:

Technological Innovation: __________________

Pros	Cons
__________	__________
__________	__________
__________	__________
__________	__________
__________	__________
__________	__________

Language for Writing

Discussing Technology

The following words and expressions are useful in discussing technological innovations. Some of them will help you write about technology in general, and others relate to specific technological fields, such as robotics. Discuss their meanings with a partner. Then add to this list any additional words you found in your research project in Part One.

NOUNS	VERBS	ADJECTIVES	EXPRESSIONS
progress	create	technological	to mark a major
robotics	produce	innovative	breakthrough in
nanotechnology	eliminate	dehumanizing	to work on a microscale
genetic engineering	contribute	economical	to be stymied by
automation	fuel	clogged	to make an impact on
a breakthrough	envision	adventageous	to capture the interest of
a drawback	deploy		to play a prominent role
a sensor	etch		to think big
an artery	progress	________	________
a valve	________	________	________
a futurist	________	________	________
a probe	________	________	________
technology	________	________	________

Using Quotations

You can support your opinions by referring to the work and ideas of others. When you use someone else's exact words, all the words *must* be placed within quotation marks ("...") and you must name the author. For example, writer Samuel Greengard believes that the revolution in nanotechnology promises "to radically change the way we live and work."

Go back to the article "Small World" and look for the quoted passage in the fourth paragraph. Then answer the following three questions.

1. Who/What is the source? That is, who said (or wrote) the quoted passage?

____

____

2. Does the quotation support the main idea of the paragraph?

Yes _____ No _____

3. Why do you think the author chose to quote this particular passage?

____

____

____

Here are three common ways of incorporating quotations into your writing:

1. According to [author] in [source], ". . . ."

   Example: According to Samuel Greengard in "Small World," the development of micromachines "promises to radically change the way we live and work."

2. According to [source] by [author], ". . . ."

   Example: According to "Small World," an article by Samuel Greengard, "Some futurists envision nanotechnology also being used to explore the deep sea in small submarines, or even to launch finger-sized rockets packed with microminiature instruments."

3. In [source], [author] says (said, states) ". . . ."

   Example: In "Small World," Samuel Greengard says that "Automobile manufacturers soon will begin using tiny devices that run on static electricity to sense when to release an airbag and how to keep engines and brakes operating efficiently."

Follow these tips when using quotations:

- Use a quotation when the author's own words have impact or cannot be improved upon. (Be careful not to overuse quotations.)
- Use the author's first and last name or only the last name. (Don't use the author's first name alone.)
- Underline or italicize book titles and the names of newspapers and magazines.
- Put quotation marks around the titles of articles.

Paraphrasing

A second way to support your ideas by referring to sources is to *paraphrase* part of an article. A paraphrase is a restatement of a phrase or sentence that is approximately as long as the original statement. Citing the source is still necessary. Although a paraphrase should be, for the most part, your *own* words, it is occasionally correct to use the author's exact words if she or he has used specialized or technical terminology for which there is no adequate synonym.

Note the following example:

Quotation: "Genetic engineering on plants will produce 'super crops' by the year 2000, including square tomatoes for easy packing and short corn stalks loaded with ears."

Source: A study done by L. William Teweles & Co.

Paraphrase: A study conducted by L. William Teweles & Co. predicts that genetic engineering will produce superior food crops such as square tomatoes by the year 2010.

Note that some of the language from the original quotation was repeated. There's only one term for "genetic engineering," and there's no adequate synonym for "produce" in this context. However, the paraphrase is clearly not the words of the study by L. William Teweles & Co. Notice also that the corn example was not included. In developing an idea, if you need a concrete detail and your original source contains one, use it. If you want to save space or time by using a paraphrase, you can do so by omitting some of the details the source contains.

Here are four tips for using paraphrases:

1. Paraphrase when it is more effective and efficient to restate the author's words in your words.
2. Don't forget to cite the source in a paraphrase.
3. If you want to save time or space by using a paraphrase, omit some of the details.
4. Use a dictionary or thesaurus to find words with similar meanings.

Practicing What You've Learned

Refer to your answer in Postreading Question 4 on page 96. Write a paragraph about some of the fields that will benefit from nanotechnology. Incorporate some quotations from paragraphs 3 and 4 of the article to support your ideas.

Write paraphrases for the following quotations about issues in advanced technology. Refer to the preceding guidelines. *Don't forget to cite the sources.*

1. *Quotation:* "Routine, repetitive, and dreary blue-collar materials-handling jobs are going to be filled by robots for less than the minimum hourly wage."
   Source: The Copely News Service
2. *Quotation:* "A new program at the Defense Advanced Research Projects Agency (DARPA) will develop computers capable of symbolic reasoning with effective computational speeds 1,000 times greater than those used in military systems today." (*Note:* Figures are like technical terminology—you can't paraphrase them.)
   Source: Robert Cooper, Director of DARPA
3. *Quotation:* "The Japanese aim to produce machines easy enough to use, and intelligent and fast enough in their responses, to come close to the kinds of transactions intelligent human beings are used to having with each other."
   Source: The Fifth Generation, by Edward Feigenbaum and Pamela McCorduck (*Note:* This is a book about the supercomputers being developed in Japan.)

Write a paragraph in which you discuss one advantage or disadvantage of a particular technological advancement. Use one quotation, and at least one paraphrase; you may want to use vocabulary from the list in Part Two, page 98. Base your writing on the ideas and sources from your research from the Gathering Information section in Part One.

Write a paragraph in which you describe one of the photos at the beginning of the chapter. You may want to use words and expressions from the list in Part Two.

PART three
Systems for Writing

> **Review Point**
>
> A thesis statement expresses the main idea of an essay.

Introductions

> **New Points**
> - An introduction is usually the first paragraph of an essay.
> - Its purpose is to prepare the reader for the essay.
> - An important part of the introduction is the thesis statement.
> - The thesis statement usually appears at the end of the introduction.

There are several ways to interest the reader in what you are going to discuss in your essay. Here are three types of introductions: general-to-specific, chronological, and problem-solution.

General-to-Specific

This type of introduction consists of two or three sentences that lead to the thesis, with each new sentence more specific than the last. This kind of introduction can be represented by an upside-down triangle:

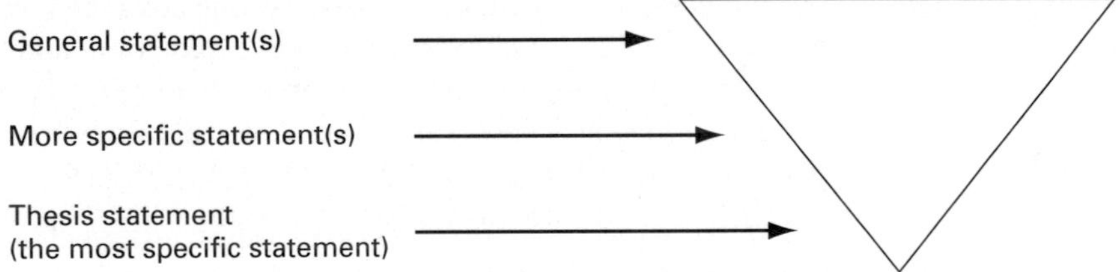

Example: There is a great deal of interest in the use of multimedia in education. Schools everywhere are purchasing CD-ROMs, laser-disk players, and sophisticated computers. Many schools have established computer resource centers and provide special training in the use of multimedia for teachers. The use of multimedia in education has important benefits for both students and teachers.

In this introduction, the reader is led on a slightly narrowing path to the specific thesis statement.

Chronological

This kind of introduction often leads chronologically into the issue the writer wants to discuss. It is almost like a story: if the writer tells the story well, the reader wants to continue reading to see what happens next, or to see how this amusing, interesting, or shocking incident relates to the essay as a whole.

Example: I bought my first tape player in 1974. It was a reel-to-reel machine, which was heavy and expensive. I only used it at home. I purchased my second tape player in 1980. It was smaller than the first, slightly less expensive, lighter in weight and much better in sound quality. It played and recorded tape cassettes. I took it overseas with me and finally gave it to some friends in Tahiti. I bought my current cassette player this year. It's bigger than my second tape recorder because it also has a radio and a compact-disc player. However, it's lighter still, and the speakers are more powerful. Advances in technology have enabled me to listen to my favorite music wherever I want and in a variety of different formats.

This introduction traces the effects of technology on this writer's personal enjoyment of music. What do you think the writer discusses in the body of this essay?

Problem-Solution

This kind of introduction begins with a short (three- to five-sentence) explanation of a problem, one that the essay will attempt to solve. The introduction ends with a solution to the problem.

Example: A recent study has shown that children watch an average of seven hours of television a day. This is a great concern to many parents. They worry that the violence on television will influence their children's behavior. They also worry that the frequent commercials for unhealthy food will affect their children's eating habits. Parents are furthermore concerned that television programs present false information that could be detrimental. What can they do? The solution to this problem is simple: Parents should carefully select the programs their children watch and limit the number of viewing hours.

Note that sometimes these types of introductions overlap. That is, an introduction might have the characteristics of more than one of the types described in this chapter.

Review Points

- Readers should be able to predict what an essay is about from the thesis statement.
- The thesis statement can also include ideas the writer will use to support his or her viewpoint.

Essay Development

New Points

- A well-developed essay has concrete, relevant details.
- Supporting paragraphs should be balanced: They should contain information of equal importance presented in equal depth.
- Ideas should flow smoothly from one paragraph to another through careful use of transitions.

Read the following essay about a technological development and then answer the questions.

There is a great deal of interest in the use of computers in education. The educational use of computers is called Computer Assisted Instruction, or CAI. Many public schools in the United States have acquired computers and CAI programs to run on them. School districts are establishing computer resource centers and special training programs to help teachers use computers. In addition, some colleges and universities are beginning to establish "computer literacy" requirements for graduation. In spite of all this interest in the use of computers in education, some educators and students still may be wondering if this expensive toy is really worth their time and, in some cases, money. The answer is a definite *yes:* The use of computers in education has important benefits for both students and teachers.

Computers enhance a student's learning experience in many ways. First of all, the computer has the ability to accommodate individual differences in learning speed because the user (the student) is the one who controls the pace of the lessons. In addition, because a computer is nonjudgmental, the learner does not have to be afraid of reprisal or humiliation when making errors. For example, because computers can repeat information over and over, the user can ask for many repetitions of a lesson without fearing a judgmental response about his or her ability to learn. The beneficial effects of learning in a stress-free atmosphere are well documented. A third advantage of CAI is that a computer can give a student immediate feedback. It can tell the student why she or he is wrong as soon as an error is made, and it can even provide an appropriate hint for figuring out the correct answer.

Not only do computers benefit students, they also make the teacher's job easier. One advantage lies in the preparation of instructional materials. Schools and colleges can purchase educational computer programs that can be adapted to any learning situation. These systems, called "authoring systems," are like skeletal lesson plans: The format of several exercises and tests is already planned out; all the teacher adds is the information he or she wants the students to learn (mathematical problems, vocabulary lists, and so forth). The authoring system automatically incorporates these teaching points into its preplanned format and then is ready to be used by several students for a long time. The system can also correct the students' work and determine and record grades. In addition, the computer offers numerous advantages to teachers in managing their classrooms. A computer laboratory (a room having one computer for every two students) can free the teacher to meet individually with students while the rest of the class is occupied with computer lessons. Finally, computers can help teachers keep student records and chart student progress, thereby cutting down on time-consuming paperwork.

With all of these advantages for both teachers and students, it is easy to see why there is so much interest in using computers in education. Of course, there are those who are skeptical and view computers as a passing fad. There are those also who simply are afraid of them. In time, however, computers will become as familiar in the classroom as chalkboards are today.

1. Look at the thesis statement. On the basis of this, what do you expect to read about in the essay? How do you expect the essay to be organized?

2. What are the supporting ideas in the thesis? Write them here:

   ____

   ____

   ____

   Are they balanced? That is, are they equally important?

   Yes _____ No _____

3. Now review the rest of the essay. How does the writer move from one paragraph to another? Are the transitions between paragraphs smooth?

4. Make a list of details the writer includes in the body paragraphs.

   ____

   ____

   ____

   ____

   Are they concrete?

   Yes _____ No _____

Are they relevant? (Do they all relate to the topic?)

Yes _____ No _____

5. Are the paragraphs of the body logically developed?

Yes _____ No _____

Do they support the thesis statement?

Yes _____ No _____

focus on testing

Checking Your Main Idea

In questions 1 and 2 in the previous exercise you were supposed to review the thesis statement and predict what you will read in the essay based on the introduction. Whenever you write under time pressure, it is a good idea to go back to the beginning and check your thesis statement before you have completed the essay. Do you discuss what the thesis statement promises? Checking your main idea will help you avoid going off-topic.

Practicing What You've Learned

Write introductions for the following thesis statements, which were written by students. Their essay topics appear in parentheses after each thesis statement.

a. Through technological innovations, life has become more convenient and comfortable, but the earth has not become a safe place to live in. (*Topic:* The Advantages and Disadvantages of Technological Innovations)

b. The solution to this problem is to allocate more money to the research and development of solar energy. (*Topic:* How Solar Energy Is Superior to Nuclear Energy)

Rewrite the introductory paragraphs from three of your previous essays. Use each of the three introduction types described in this chapter.

The following is an incomplete draft of an essay about the advantages and disadvantages of technology in general. The draft lacks specific details. Rewrite the introduction and complete the essay so that it conforms to the description of a well-developed essay.

Technology is around us every day. We see examples of advanced technology at work, at home, in the city, and even in the country. Although technology has brought us many useful things, such as improved living conditions, it has also brought us disadvantages, such as air pollution.

As a result of technological innovation, our living conditions have improved dramatically. . . .

Air pollution is one of the negative results of advanced technology. . . .

Hint: Correct the thesis statement first. You may also want to make the transitions between paragraphs smoother.

Brainstorming before starting an essay is the best way to generate specific, concrete, and relevant details to develop your ideas for writing. Refer to the brainstorming hints in step 2, Exercise 3, page 87. As a class or in groups, choose one of the following assignments and brainstorm for ideas. Take notes. Then write the essay on your own.

Writing Assignments

Write an essay on one of the following topics. Use new vocabulary and expressions you learned in this chapter, and make sure that your paragraphs are clear and coherent. Develop your ideas by using information from the research you did in Part One.

1. Discuss the advantages and/or disadvantages of one aspect of advanced technology. You can choose an example of advanced technology from the following list or think of one on your own.
   - **a.** military/weapons technology
   - **b.** the personal computer
   - **c.** nuclear energy
   - **d.** bioengineering (as it relates to agriculture or genetics)
   - **e.** Computer Assisted Instruction
   - **f.** robotics
   - **g.** nanotechnology
2. Discuss the causes or effects of a technological advancement. Use the preceding list for examples.
3. Discuss the impact of one technological advancement on your home country or city.
4. Write an essay in answer to the following question: In general, has technology done more harm than good?
5. Respond to the following quotation: "In these days of urban decay and energy crisis, there is a constant longing to return to the land and flee back to a simpler way of life. But it can't be done." —*Isaac Asimov*

6. Write an essay about a technological issue that interests you.

PART four
Evaluating for Rewriting

Working with Your Partner

step 1

Exchange the essays you wrote for the Writing Assignments section. Use the following questionnaire to evaluate each other's essays.

1. Read only the introduction (the first paragraph). Does it make you want to read the rest of the essay?

   Yes _____ No _____

   Explain why or why not.

   ____

   ____

2. Locate the thesis statement. On the basis of your understanding of the thesis, what do you expect to read about in the essay? How do you expect the essay to be organized? Explain briefly in the following space:

   ____

   ____

   ____

3. What are the supporting ideas in the thesis statement? Write them here:

   ____

   ____

   ____

   Are they balanced? That is, are they equally important?

   Yes _____ No _____

   If the answer is *no,* make suggestions for improvement.

   ____

   ____

   ____

4. Read the rest of the essay. Does the writer move smoothly from one paragraph to another?

   Yes _____ No _____

If the answer is *no,* make suggestions for improving the writer's transitions between paragraphs.

5. Make a list of details the writer includes in the body of the essay.

_______________ _______________

_______________ _______________

_______________ _______________

Are they concrete?

Yes _____ No _____

If the answer is *no,* make suggestions for improvement.

____

____

____

Are the supporting ideas relevant?

Yes _____ No _____

If the answer is *no,* make suggestions for improvement.

____

____

____

Return each other's essays. Read your partner's evaluation of your essay. Discuss any questions you have with your partner.

Working on Your Own

Now you should be ready to evaluate your own essay. Go through the questions again. Take into consideration what your partner said about your essay development when he or she evaluated it. Are your supporting ideas balanced? Are the paragraphs of the body adequately developed? Is anything missing?

step 2

Rewrite your essay, making any necessary changes. Turn this revised draft of your essay in to your teacher.

CHAPTER SIX

Money Matters

in this chapter

You will research a successful business person and write about the qualities and characteristics that can lead to success in business.

PART one
Ideas for Writing

Getting Started

What does it take to start your own business and make it a success? Personality? Location? A good product? Timing? Higher education or specialized training? In this chapter, you're going to think about the personal qualities and conditions that contribute to a successful business. You're also going to learn about some people who started successful companies—all immigrants, and all in businesses related to technology.

Read these facts about some immigrants to the United States who founded successful high-tech companies in Silicon Valley, California. Then answer the questions that follow.

THE FOUNDERS

Philippe Kahn
NATIVE COUNTRY: France
YEAR EMIGRATED TO UNITED STATES: 1982
AGE AT THE TIME: 30
NAME OF COMPANY: Borland International Inc.
WHAT IT DOES: Spreadsheets, databases, and tool software
NUMBER OF LOCAL EMPLOYEES: 1,100
MOST RECENT ANNUAL SALES: $464 million

Amr Mohsen
NATIVE COUNTRY: Egypt
YEAR EMIGRATED TO UNITED STATES: 1970
AGE AT THE TIME: 23
NAME OF COMPANY: Aptix Corp.
WHAT IT DOES: Designs field programmable components
NUMBER OF LOCAL EMPLOYEES: 65
MOST RECENT ANNUAL SALES: Not available

Winston Chen
NATIVE COUNTRY: Taiwan
YEAR EMIGRATED TO UNITED STATES: 1965
AGE AT THE TIME: 24
NAME OF COMPANY: Solectron Corp.
WHAT IT DOES: Circuit card assembly
NUMBER OF LOCAL EMPLOYEES: 3,000
MOST RECENT ANNUAL SALES: $800 million

Pauline Lo Alker
NATIVE COUNTRY: China
YEAR EMIGRATED TO UNITED STATES: 1960
AGE AT THE TIME: 17
NAME OF COMPANY: Network Peripherals Inc.
WHAT IT DOES: Makes devices to control computer networks
NUMBER OF LOCAL EMPLOYEES: 43
MOST RECENT ANNUAL SALES: Approximately $10 million

1. Scan the information about the high-tech company founders again and fill in the following chart:

founder name	company name	number of employees	most recent annual sales
1. ______	______	______	______
2. ______	______	______	______
3. ______	______	______	______
4. ______	______	______	______

2. Look at the chart you just made. Which company has the greatest number of employees? ______________________

____

3. Which company has the highest sales figures? ______________________

____

4. To decide which company is the most successful, what additional information about the companies do you need? ______________________

____

____

Brainstorming

In small groups, discuss what a business has to be or do in order to be successful. Does success mean the company has high sales figures or a large number of employees? Or does it mean something else? Consider these factors as you discuss:

1. The company contributes to the local economy.
2. The company has happy employees (employees who stay with the company a long time).
3. The company is socially and environmentally responsible (it doesn't harm people or the environment.)
4. The company has a diverse workforce (a balance of males and females, and employees from different cultures).

Write your definition of a successful business here: ______________________________

____

Freewriting

Describe what you consider to be a successful business. Write for five minutes without stopping. To get started, think about a company you know that has been very successful. Use some of the ideas you discussed in Brainstorming on the previous page.

Reading for Ideas

The following news story about immigrants who have founded successful Silicon Valley companies appeared in the business section of *The San Francisco Examiner.* Answer the following questions in small groups before you read.

1. Do you think it would be difficult for an immigrant to the United States or Canada to start his or her own company? Consider the steps he or she might have to take, how many years it might take, what obstacles he or she might encounter, etc.
2. Where is Silicon Valley? What is it known for? Name some Silicon Valley companies and the products or services they provide.
3. What is a "start-up" company?
4. What is "revenue?"

Valley Visionaries: A World of Talent
Foreign-born entrepreneurs make area a tech leader

By Tom Abate, Examiner Technology Writer

Like many immigrants, Philippe Kahn came to California intending to overstay his tourist visa and find a job, disregarding the rules foreigners must follow to work in the United States.

But for the French-born founder of Borland International Inc., this story of illegal immigration ended happily. Today the 41-year-old Kahn employs 1,100 people in the Scotts Valley headquarters of the software company he founded and built into a $500 million a year global organization.

Kahn recalls that four years after his arrival in 1982, when Borland already had 500 employees and $100 million in sales, the Immigration and Naturalization Service began questioning his status.

"At that time, I was still not a legal alien," admitted the software engineer. He had to hire an attorney to prove that, as Borland's founder, he was doing a job no American could perform—a requirement for getting a permit to work here.

Kahn's story, though colorful, is hardly unique in Silicon Valley. Foreign-born executives are common at the highest ranks of U.S. firms—people like German-born Michael Spindler, CEO (chief executive officer) of Apple Computer, Inc., Wim Roelandts, the Belgian who runs Hewlett-Packard's computer division, and Albert Yu, a native of Shanghai who heads Intel Corp 's microprocessor division.

At a time when many Americans are debating whether immigration is a blessing or a burden, the number of high-tech firms founded by immigrants demonstrates that newcomers have created jobs and revenue for Silicon Valley.

"The ability of Silicon Valley to attract the best and the brightest from around the world is one of the reasons the region has remained a technology leader," said William Hasler, dean of the business school at the University of California at Berkeley.

In an informal survey, *The Examiner* located 21 foreign-born executives who founded or helped start more than 25 Silicon Valley companies with combined annual sales exceeding $4.7 billion.

These companies range from 65-person outfits like Aptix Corp., a semiconductor start-up founded by Egyptian-born Amr Mohsen, to giant firms like Solectron Corp., headed by Taiwanese-born chairman Winston Chen, which employs 3,000 people.

"From a technology standpoint, Silicon Valley is the best place in the world to start a new high-tech business," said Chen, who came to the United States in 1965 as a 24-year old student.

Today, Chen oversees a company that did about $800 million worth of business in circuit card assembly in 1993. The 52-year old Chen said Silicon Valley is enriched by the talent of immigrants from around the world.

According to venture capitalist and former semiconductor engineer Pierre Lamond, "Silicon Valley is perhaps the easiest place in the world to launch a high-tech start-up." Lamond exported his own engineering skills from France in 1957, and later became part of the team that revived National Semiconductor in 1967.

Lamond said private investors in Silicon Valley, unlike those in Europe, are eager to invest in start-ups. "Risk-takers are rewarded and looked up to here," Lamond said. "People who try to break the mold are not regarded highly in a conservative country like Germany or France."

Hasler, of U.C.–Berkeley, said the Europeans in Silicon Valley tend to start their careers as employees of U.S. subsidiaries in Europe and eventually transfer to the headquarters, where some of them end up branching out on their own.

Immigrants from others parts of the world tend to follow a different path, Hasler said, often coming to the United States as college students who stay to find work.

Consider the experience of Pauline Lo Alker, whose family fled to Hong Kong from China after the communist takeover in 1949. In 1960, she came to the United States as a 17-year-old to study music, math, and computing. She graduated from college in 1965 but had trouble finding work in a computer industry dominated by men.

"I figured if I couldn't get in the front door, I'd get in the back door," said Alker, who took a job as a secretary, then demonstrated her skill in programming and began climbing the corporate ladder.

Today, the 50-year-old Alker is CEO of Network Peripherals, a 43-person, $10 million business. Alker, who had already founded and sold another start-up, Counterpoint Computers Inc., calls herself "a believer in the American dream."

"Immigrants have always provided energy and vitality," she said. "The race and color is shifting with this new set of immigrants from Asia and Latin America, but we are still Americans."

Tom Abate

postreading questions

1. What are some contributions immigrant entrepreneurs (people who start businesses) have made to Silicon Valley?

2. Why is Silicon Valley a good place for an immigrant to launch a high-tech business?

3. In paragraph 13, Pierre Lamond says that unlike American investors, investors in some European countries don't value risk-takers. From what you know of these countries and cultures, discuss whether you agree or disagree with him. Name some other countries/cultures that do not value risk-taking and some that do.

4. Explain the difference between the way European and non-European immigrants tend to find success in business in Silicon Valley, according to William Hasler. How do the situations of Kahn and Alker support Hasler's ideas?

5. What is "the American Dream?" How is Alker an example of the American Dream?

6. Do you know of any other recent immigrants who have founded successful businesses? If so, share your information with your classmates.

7. Would you like to start your own company? Why or why not? If your answer is "yes," what kind of business would it be? Would you start it in your home country or in another country? Why? ______________________

____

____

____

8. Think about the personal qualities, characteristics, or backgrounds of a successful business person. With a partner, make a list of characteristics and qualities that help a person succeed in business. When you are finished, compare your list with the following list of possible answers.

____

____

____

POSSIBLE ANSWERS

luck, intelligence, persistence, experience, a good education

training, confidence, motivation, money, a willingness to take risks

THINKING CRITICALLY

Speculating

"Speculating" means figuring out what you do not know based on what you do know. Work in small groups and *speculate* about the causes of success. Compare Alker and Kahn, based on what you know about them from the article or from other information you might have about them, and speculate about the following:

Which person probably had an easier time starting a business? Why? Consider such things as gender, background, country of origin, etc. List the factors that may have contributed to or hindered their success:

____

____

____

____

Gathering Information

Choose one of the entrepreneurs listed in "The Founders" on pages 112 and 113 and find out as much as you can about the person and the business he or she founded. Go to the library and use the following sources of information. Take notes on the information you gather and organize the notes in a summary that you will share with your teacher and classmates.

POSSIBLE SOURCES ARE:

1. The reference librarian
2. The card or computer catalog, especially if the businessperson is no longer alive
3. The *Reader's Guide to Periodical Literature,* a general index, an especially good source of information on people who are still living
4. The *Business Periodicals Index,* an index to business publications, also a good source of information on people who are still living

You may also choose one of these noted entrepreneurs from America's past, or any other entrepreneur who interests you:

1. Ray Kroc (1902–1984)
   President
   McDonald Corporation
2. Levi Strauss (1829–1902)
   Founder
   Levi Strauss & Co.
3. A. P. Giannini (1870–1949)
   Founder
   Bank of America
4. C. J. Walker (1867–1919)
   Inventor, Entrepreneur
   Cosmetics

PART two
Language for Writing

Discussing Success in Business

The following words and expressions from "Valley Visionaries" are useful in describing businesses and business people. Find each word and expression in the article and study its meaning in the context of the news story. Discuss the meanings with a partner.

NOUNS	VERBS	IDIOMS
risk-takers	to perform	to get in the front/back door
energy	to take risks	to break the mold
venture capitalist	to branch out	to look up to someone

NOUNS	VERBS	IDIOMS
vitality	to found } a business	to climb the corporate ladder
talent	to run } a business	
start-up	to head } a business	
revenue	to launch } a business	
the best and the brightest	to create jobs	

Based on information in the article "Valley Visionaries," the statistics in "The Founders," and your answer to Postreading Question 8, organize new words you learned into two lists that describe successful entrepreneurs (such as Kahn, Alker, Mohsen, and Chen) and successful businesses (such as Borland International or Network Peripherals). The first one is done as an example.

SUCCESSFUL ENTREPRENEURS	SUCCESSFUL BUSINESSES
energetic	profitable

Practicing What You've Learned

exercise 1 Rewrite your description of successful businesses from Freewriting, Part One, using expressions and vocabulary from this section.

Imagine that you and your classmates are members of a very successful import-export company. In a paragraph, describe the individual members of this company and recent events by using language from this section.

In a paragraph, describe a successful businessperson that you know. Provide as many details as possible to explain this person's success.

With a partner, write a paragraph about one of the entrepreneurs in Part One. Try to do this from memory, using new words and expressions from this section.

Does success in other areas (education, fine arts, sports) require the same qualities as success in business? Write a one-paragraph response to this question using specific examples.

PART three
Systems for Writing

Review Points

- A paragraph must develop one main idea.
- The main idea is often in the first sentence of a paragraph.
- The rest of the paragraph explains, illustrates, and expands the main idea.

Paragraph Coherence Through Pronouns, Key Words, and Paraphrasing

New Points

- A paragraph is easier to read if the sentences in it all move smoothly from one to the other. This is called *coherence*.
- Coherence means a "logical or natural connection."
- Writers achieve coherence through the use of pronouns, repetition of key words, and paraphrases.

Following are examples of how writers use pronouns, repetition of key words, and paraphrases to achieve coherence.

Writers use *pronouns* to refer to nouns already mentioned.

Example: Consider the experience of Pauline Lo Alker, whose family fled to Hong Kong from China after the communist takeover in 1949. In 1960, *she* came to the United States as a 17-year-old to study music, math, and computing. *She* graduated from college in 1965, but had trouble finding work in a computer industry dominated by men.

They use repetition of *keywords* and *concepts,* which are carefully chosen words and expressions that develop the writer's point.

Example: A *willingness to take risks* is one of the most important qualities that leads to success in business. A person who is *willing to take risks* is one who, despite the possibility of failure, will move ahead in a new business venture with confidence in his or her abilities.

Note: Be careful not to overuse repetition; if you do, your writing may become simple and uninteresting.

Writers also use *paraphrases,* which are restatements of words or expressions from a previous sentence. Paraphrases reduce repetition of key words and phrases but establish coherence by reminding the reader of the important points.

Example: Lamond said private investors in Silicon Valley, unlike those in Europe, are eager to invest in start-ups. "*Risk-takers* are rewarded and looked up to here," Lamond said. "*People who try to break the mold* are not regarded highly in a conservative country like Germany or France."

Review Points

- An introduction prepares the reader for the essay.
- One kind of introduction is the general-to-specific; its form is like an upside down triangle

Conclusions

New Points

- A conclusion prepares the reader for the end of your essay, giving her or him a feeling of completion.
- A specific-to-general conclusion—the most common type—begins with a restatement of your thesis and then moves on to two or three increasingly general statements on the topic as a whole.

Study this example of a conclusion:

> So it is trust in oneself that assures success when starting a new business. In fact, this confidence allows people to succeed in more than just business. Whether it is learning a new skill or meeting a new friend, certainty about one's abilities makes everything easier. Confidence brings success to all parts of one's life.

Notice how the examples in the conclusion move from specific to general.

Practicing What You've Learned

In the paragraphs below, the key concepts in the topic sentences have been circled. Read each paragraph carefully, find the words and expressions that recall the key concepts, and underline them.

A. Public accounting consists largely of auditing and tax services. An *audit* is a review of the financial records of an organization. Auditing is usually performed at fixed intervals of time—perhaps quarterly, semiannually, or annually. And as the tax laws have grown increasingly complex, not only corporations but also individuals have had to utilize the services of accountants in preparing their tax forms. Businesses, government agencies, and nonprofit organizations all employ public accountants either regularly or on a part-time basis.*

B. Leading executives in the best-run U.S. companies share the quality of being able not only to establish strong corporate values, but also to live according to those values. These leaders have the ability to transmit the essential qualities of their companies to other people. We describe that sort of leadership as a "value-driven style." A good example of this type of top executive is J. Willard Marriott, Sr., founder of the Marriott Corporation, who was still reading every single complaint card that came into that lodging and restaurant company until he was over eighty years old.†

Read the following paragraphs carefully. Locate the key concepts in the topic sentences and circle them. Then identify the words and expressions that recall the key concepts by underlining them.

A. Nations use the capital of other nations to build their industrial bases. This capital is used to build factories and develop mines, among other things. For example, the railroads of the United States and South America were built by British capital. This capital paid for the costs of construction, including materials, the wages of the workers, and the locomotives and freight cars. More recently, American, Japanese, and European corporations have provided funds to explore for oil and to build new automobile, steel, and chemical plants around the world.‡

B. Shaklee Corporation is one of the most successful companies in San Francisco because the managers understand the importance of giving both within and outside the corporation. It is successful because top-level management cares about the welfare of their employees as well as the com-

---

* Adapted from Sandra Costinett, *The Language of Accounting in English* (New York: Regents Publishing Company, 1977), pp. 5–6.

† Adapted from "Well-Run Companies: The Secret of Success," an interview with Thomas Peters (coauthor of *In Search of Excellence*), *U.S. News & World Report* (Oct. 10, 1983), pp. 74–75.

‡ Adapted from Peter K. Oppenheim, *The Language of International Finance in English: Money and Banking* (New York: Regents Publishing Company, 1976), p. 7.

munity in which they do business. Their employees have access to free fruit-juice bars and the use of the company's indoor health facility with its 8,000-square foot track and cardiovascular clinic. Once a year the headquarters close for the day so employees can spend it at Golden Gate Park participating in athletic events. Shaklee Corporation gives to the community as well. They sponsored the Adopt-an-Animal program at the San Francisco Zoo. They helped keep the Golden Gate Park Band alive by sponsoring the musicians for one month of the year and enlisting eleven other companies as monthly sponsors.*

The following is a topic sentence with the key concepts underlined. Write a paragraph that supports it. Use synonymous words and phrases wherever possible to recall the key concepts in the topic sentence. Underline the synonymous key words and phrases when you have finished.

example: A person who <u>achieves success in business</u> in a short amount of time is usually <u>hard working and highly motivated</u>.

To paraphrase, you must be able to use synonymous words and phrases for repeated ideas. Practice paraphrasing by providing synonyms in the right column.

1. revenues ____________________
2. entrepreneur ____________________
3. business ____________________
4. to succeed ____________________
5. flexibility ____________________
6. customers ____________________
7. employer ____________________

* Adapted from "Executive Comment," San Francisco Business (San Francisco Chamber of Commerce: September 1983).

Restate the following sentences using synonymous phrases or complete sentences. Compare answers with your classmates when you finish.

1. He gets along well with his business associates. ____________________

   ____

2. He lives for money. ____

   ____

3. She is a natural salesperson. ______________________________

   ____

4. She was in the right place at the right time. ____________________

   ____

Rewrite the following paragraphs so that they are more coherent. Repeat key words and ideas to remind the reader of the main idea; use pronouns and paraphrases to reduce repetition.

A. In Mexico one of the most important elements for success in the business world is the relationships you have. You may be a good student and a diligent worker, but you still need relationships. If you don't have good relationships, you may not even be able to find a job. And if you don't have good relationships once you've found a job, you may not be able to move up in the company. Good relationships influence how much money you make too. So establishing good relationships is extremely important for people who want to succeed in business in Mexico.

B. The most successful people are stubborn and inflexible. They insist on doing things their way. It is their stubbornness and inflexibility that allows them to maintain high standards and not compromise. Stubbornness and inflexibility allow Mrs. Field's to sell only cookies that are soft and warm. Stubbornness and inflexibility push Burger King to flame-broil their burgers. Stubbornness and inflexibility lead to success.

Following are the first sentences of four different conclusions. Working in small groups, discuss some additional, more specific ideas each conclusion could contain. Then complete each conclusion, using the ideas you discussed.

1. In conclusion, it's who you know rather than what you know that determines how far you will progress in your political career.
2. Top executives of large corporations agree that carefully listening to potential customers brings success.
3. In conclusion, there is more to life than earning a great deal of money and obtaining a position of power.
4. Therefore, starting a small business is an excellent way for a new citizen to earn a living in the United States.

Rewrite the conclusions for at least two of your previous essays. Keep in mind what you've learned in this chapter.

focus on testing

Avoiding Repetition

Exercises 4 and 5 ask you to paraphrase words and expressions. Paraphrasing improves paragraph coherence and helps you avoid repetition, making your writing sound more fluent and sophisticated. Whenever you have to write an essay on a standardized test, skim your writing for repeated words and expressions, cross them out, and write in synonymous words and phrases.

Writing Assignments

Write an essay on one of the following topics. Use new vocabulary and expressions you learned in this chapter and make sure that your paragraphs are clear and coherent. Develop your ideas by using information from the research you did in Part One.

1. Write about a successful entrepreneur who you know or have studied. Describe the factors that have contributed to his or her success.
2. Choose two personal qualities or characteristics of a successful businessperson and explain why they lead to success in the business world. Support your thesis by using information you gathered in Part One.
3. Choose a successful company and discuss some important factors that have led to its success.
4. Discuss the contribution immigrants have made to a particular area in the United States or Canada, such as Silicon Valley, or in your native country.
5. Explain, agree, or disagree with Pierre Lamond's statement that it's easier to start a high-tech business in the United States than in some other countries.
6. Explain, agree, or disagree with the following quotation: "Success in business depends more on *who* you know than on *what* you know."

7. Write an essay about any issue related to business that interests you.

PART four
Evaluating for Rewriting

Working with Your Partner

step 1

Exchange the essays you wrote for the Writing Assignments section. Use the following questionnaire to evaluate each other's essays.

1. Underline the topic sentence. What are the key concepts?

   Paragraph 1 ______________________________

   Paragraph 2 ______________________________

   Paragraph 3 ______________________________

2. Does the writer reduce repetition by providing paraphrases?

   Paragraph 1 yes _____ no _____

   Paragraph 2 yes _____ no _____

   Paragraph 3 yes _____ no _____

3. Can you give any recommendations to help the writer make his or her paragraphs more coherent? ______________________________

   ____

   ____

4. Look at the conclusion. Does it move from specific to general and leave you with a sense of completion?

   Yes _____ No _____

Return each other's essays. Read your partner's evaluation of your essay. Discuss any questions you have with your partner.

Working on Your Own

Now you should be ready to evaluate your own paper. Go through the questions again. Take into consideration what your partner said about your paper when he or she evaluated it. Is there more to add? Are there words to change?

Rewrite your essay, making any necessary changes. Turn this revised draft of your essay in to your teacher.

CHAPTER seven
Leisure Time

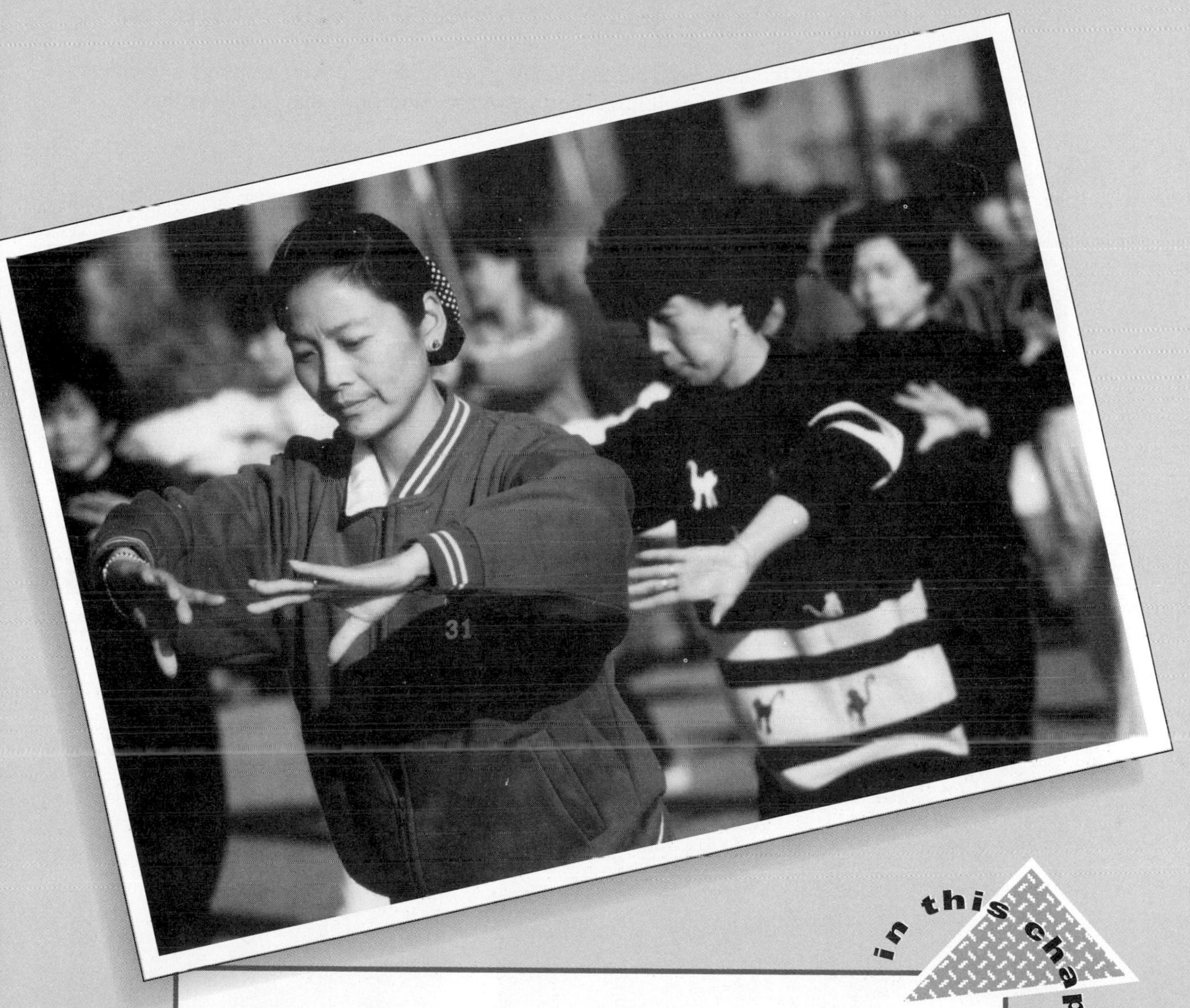

in this chapter

You will interview people about how they spend their leisure time and write about leisure-time activities that interest you.

PART one
Ideas for Writing

Getting Started

How often do you have free time? What do you like to do? Do you spend your free time alone or with others?

Look at the following photos showing people doing different things in their leisure time. Study the photos. Then answer the questions that follow with a partner.

1.

2.

4.

3.

5. 

1. How are the people in the photos using their leisure time?

2. Which of the activities do you enjoy?

3. Which of the activities do people in your home country do in their leisure time?

4. Which of the activities are passive? Which are active?

5. Which activities are done with other people? Which are done alone?

6. Which activities are done at home? Which are done away from home?

7. Which activities require training and which do not?

8. Which cost money and which do not?

9. Which are educational and which are entertaining?

Brainstorming

Make a list of the activities you like to do in your free time. Use the photos of leisure-time activities to get you started. Then, with a partner, fill in the Venn diagram.

LEISURE-TIME ACTIVITIES YOU LIKE

____

____

____

____

____

____

____

____

Activities you like to do

Activities both of you like to do

Activities your partner likes to do

Look at the photos and your list and think of characteristic features that describe at least two of the activities. We'll call these categories. Refer to the questions on page 129, but think of additional categories also. Write the categories below. One category is given as an example.

CATEGORIES

passive

____

____

____

____

Complete the chart by choosing three categories, listing the categories in the boxes, and writing the corresponding activities in the column below each box. Some of the activities may fall into more than one category. We've provided one category.

passive		
watching TV		
sleeping		
listening to music		
reading		

Freewriting

Write for fifteen minutes about your favorite leisure-time activity. Why do you prefer it to other activities? Does it require a special skill? How did you learn it? Who first taught you to do it? Do you do it with others or alone?

Reading for Ideas

Some people spend their free time participating in sports. Others prefer to watch athletes, either at the event or on TV. The reading selection in this chapter is about a sports festival that people all over the world wait for and watch. Answer the following questions before you read.

prereading questions

1. What are the Olympic Games?
2. How often do they occur?
3. When and where will the next Olympic Games take place?
4. What are some of the events?
5. What events have athletes from your country participated in? In which events have athletes from your country been particularly successful?
6. Which are your favorite Olympic events? Why?
7. As you read this article, note the organization of ideas in the passage. What two main categories of information does it contain? What examples describe each category?

The Olympic Games

The Olympic Games are an international sports festival that began in 776 B.C. in ancient Greece. They took place every four years for hundreds of years until they were discontinued at the end of the 4th century A.D. In 1896, the Olympic Games began again and have continued to take place every fourth year, except in 1916, 1940, and 1944 during World Wars I and II. Since 1992, Summer Games and Winter Games alternate every two years.

For the ancient Greeks, the Olympic Games were a way of honoring their gods. All wars would cease during these games. There were theater performances and competition in music and oratory as well as in athletic events. The modern Olympics honor the athletic talents of citizens of all countries. They are always held in a different host nation and begin with a runner who carries a blazing torch into the arena to light the Olympic flame. They last for two-and-a-half weeks and promote friendly competition in place of international conflict.

The Olympics have grown from ten to more than twenty-one sports in the past hundred years. Women were first allowed to participate in 1912. A separate series of winter games started in 1924, so now the athletic events are divided into summer and winter games. The summer Olympics are subdivided into five areas: track and field sports, gymnasium competition, water sports, team events, and horseback riding competition. There are several different contests for each of these divisions, including archery, basketball, boxing, canoeing and kayaking, cycling, equestrian arts, fencing, swimming, diving, synchronized swimming, track and field, volleyball, water polo, weight lifting, wrestling, and yachting.

Unlike the summer games, the winter Olympics are always held in a mountainous country where there is plenty of snow. The slopes and snowy weather conditions are necessary for winter events, which include skiing, ice-skating, and team sports. Skiers compete in four kinds of events: jumping events, downhill and cross-country races, and the slalom. The slalom is a steep downhill race over a zigzag course. There are two types of skating events: speed skating and figure skating. Speed skating involves racing on the ice against other skaters or the clock. In figure skating, skaters—individually or in pairs—perform intricate routines on the ice, involving athletic movements and dance. Team sports include ice hockey and bobsledding events. In the two types of bobsledding events, either two- or four-person teams race their sleds over icy courses.

The International Olympic Committee (IOC) in Lausanne, Switzerland, governs the Games. Recently, the need for a governing board has grown stronger because the Games have become an arena where personal and political aspirations are sometimes played out. For example, the governing board had a widely publicized role during the 1994 Winter Olympics after figure skater Tonya Harding's alleged assault on rival skater Nancy Kerrigan.

The Harding–Kerrigan case, however, was unusual. The Olympics are internationally popular not because of the personal conflicts that sometimes develop, but because people like to see their countries represented in an international arena. Because some of the best athletes in the world compete, the events provide a thrilling spectacle.

postreading questions

1. Organize the information from the reading selection about the types of Olympic events by filling in the following organizational chart. There are boxes for the two *main* types of events and for all the smaller categories. See how many boxes you can fill in without looking back at the reading selection. Note that the chart corresponds to an outline that lists general points first and less general, or specific, points next. The most general information goes in boxes marked with a **I.**, while the most specific information goes in boxes marked **1.**, **2.**, **3.**, **4.** The more specific the information, the greater the indentation. Two examples are done for you.

THE OLYMPIC GAMES

I. Summer Games
- **A.** track and field
- **B.**
- **C.**
- **D.**
- **E.**

I.
- **A.**
  - **1.**
  - **2.**
  - **3.**
  - **4.**
- **B.**
  - **1.**
  - **2.**
- **C.**
  - **1.**
  - **2.**

2. Look up any new words in the selection and write their meanings.

3. Reread the selection and underline the words and expressions that show how the information is *categorized.* Write the expressions below. The first one is done for you.

a. are divided into

b. ______

c. ______

Discuss these questions with two or three classmates:

4. Have you ever attended the Olympic Games? Where and when?

5. When were the last summer Olympics? Winter Olympics? Where did they take place?______

6. Are the Olympics important to sports fans in your country? Has your country ever hosted the Olympics?______

7. Can you think of any Olympic champions from either your country or another?______

THINKING CRITICALLY

Distinguishing Between General and Specific Information

In "The Olympic Games," you read both general and specific information about the Olympics. Understanding the relationship between *general* and *specific* information is an important critical thinking skill.

Look at the following pairs of words and review their relationship.

- Insert > between the words if the word or phrase on the left is more general than the word or phrase on the right.
- Insert < between the words if the word or phrase on the left is more specific than the word or phrase on the right.
- Insert = between the words if they are equal in terms of generality.

The first one is done as an example.

Olympics	>	Summer Olympics
downhill skiing	________	figure skating
winter events	________	summer events
winter events	________	slalom
weight lifting	________	gymnasium competition
cycling	________	Summer Olympics
team events	________	water sports
ice skating	________	speed skating

Gathering Information

Leisure time in the United States and Canada is highly valued. How do your American or Canadian friends and acquaintances spend their leisure time? Ask two Americans or Canadians what they like to do most in their leisure time and why they prefer this activity. Share your results with the class. Do you see any relationship(s) between choice of activities and the age, sex, or occupation of the people you interviewed? For example, do men prefer certain activities and women others?

name	age	sex (M/F)	occupation	activity	why activity is enjoyed
1.					
2.					
3.					
4.					

Language for Writing

Classifying Leisure-Time Activities

Often in academic and scientific writing, students have to organize information into groups or classes. Study the following expressions, which are useful in classifying information. Note the underlined word endings.

Leisure-time activities	can be { divided / classified / grouped / subdivided / organized / placed / categorized }	into (number)	{ categories. / subcategories. / groups. / subdivisions. / classes. / types. / areas. }
Leisure-time activities	fall into (number)	{ categories. / groups. / classes. }	
There are (number)	{ types / kinds } of leisure-time activities		

Other examples:

- Winter sports can be divided into five categories.
- The museums in my town fall into two groups.
- There are at least two kinds of figure skating activities.

Reviewing Countable and Uncountable Nouns

Remember that single countable nouns must be preceded by either the definite article (*the*) or the indefinite article (*a* or *an*).

Incorrect: Athletes need supportive *environment* in order to become successful.

Correct: Athletes need *a* supportive *environment* in order to become successful.

Correct: His success as an athlete was a result of *the* supportive environment his family and friends provided.

Uncountable nouns cannot appear with *a* or *an*, and they have no plural form.

Incorrect: *Progresses* in athletic ability *are* often the result of professional coaching.

Correct: *Progress* in athletic ability *is* often the result of professional coaching.

Go back to Part One and quickly reread the selection "The Olympic Games." Underline as many nouns as you can while you read; then use these nouns to complete the following exercise. Work with a classmate. List at least ten countable nouns below. Include the article for singular nouns. Here are three examples.

athletes

a nation

the arena

List at least *three uncountable* nouns below. One is given as an example.

snow

____

____

____

____

Practicing What You've Learned

Refer to the reading selection on the Olympic Games in Part One. Write one or more paragraphs about further subdivisions of the five types of summer Olympic events. Below are some ideas to help you get started. Add additional information you might know about these events. Study the following example, and brainstorm for ideas and information with your class before you start.

TRACK AND FIELD SPORTS	GYMNASIUM COMPETITION	TEAM EVENTS	WATER SPORTS	RIDING COMPETITION
races	fencing	basketball	swimming	horsemanship
jumping	gymnastics	volleyball	rowing	cycling
decathlon	weight lifting		yachting	

example: Water sports in the summer Olympics can be divided into three areas: rowing, swimming, and yachting. The rowing events usually take place in a natural lake, and they are beautiful to watch. The swimming events are held in an indoor or outdoor pool and include individual and team competitions. The yachting events are my favorite, because I enjoy watching the different boats.

A sociologist at a large university recently did a study of how students spend their free time. The most popular categories of leisure-time activities follow. Using the classification expressions on page 138, write a paragraph about one of the categories. Subdivide the general category into three more specific classes based on your knowledge and experience. Study the example before you begin.

CATEGORIES

Museums	Vehicles used for recreation
Television programs	Music
Reading materials	Movies
Sports	Food
Vacations	

example: There are three types of museums in my hometown: art, natural history, and anthropology. I prefer to visit natural history museums because there are often many displays of animals in their natural habitats. The displays are interesting and I always learn something from them.

Visit the library in your school or community. Write a paragraph explaining how the books are organized. Use language from this section.

There are several mistakes in the sentences below. Correct as many as you can, keeping in mind the rules for countable and uncountable nouns reviewed in this section.

1. Athlete can become successful when they have an adequate training facilities, a knowledgeable coaches, and a balanced and nutritious diet. (There are three mistakes.)
2. I had some free time last summer, so I decided to accept job at popular pizza restaurant. This work was very stressful because many times I had to deal with difficult customer and hectic work atmosphere. (There are four mistakes.)
3. Maria's father taught her how to take pictures when she was child, and photography has been her hobby ever since. Although she specializes in portraits of children, she also likes to photograph flower, tree, and natural scene. (There are four mistakes.)

PART three
Systems for Writing

Review Points

- Pronouns, key words and paraphrasing can help you create paragraph coherence.
- A conclusion is the opposite of an introduction. It ends the essay.

Writing Well-Developed Paragraphs

New Points

- To make your writing interesting and convincing, you need to develop your ideas logically and thoroughly. You want to avoid writing superficial paragraphs—that is, paragraphs in which the ideas are not carefully developed or fully explained. Superficial writing leaves the reader with many questions. Well-developed writing tries to answer as many of the reader's questions as possible.
- To write a well-developed paragraph, first try to predict all the questions a reader may have. Then answer the questions by:
  - Explaining or paraphrasing your ideas
  - Providing facts
  - Giving examples
  - Adding specific details
  - Doing a combination of these things

The following two paragraphs about leisure-time activities aren't as well developed as they could be. First, read the paragraphs.

A. Lee was the most successful swimmer in his hometown because he had many physical advantages. First, he was taller than most of his competitors. Second, he had big hands, large feet, and long limbs. These physical advantages gave him confidence. It is not surprising that he was the best swimmer in his hometown.

B. Traveling is not only a good way for people to relax and escape the pressure of daily routines, but it is also very educational. Traveling teaches people a lot about other cultures. Visiting other places can also improve communication skills. Finally, traveling can make a person interested in studying at a college or university. Traveling is a good way to learn.

Now, look at the questions in the charts on the facing page to see how the writer can further develop the paragraphs.

sentence	question
1. Lee was the most successful swimmer in his hometown because he had many physical advantages.	What advantages?
2. First, he was taller than most of his competitors.	Why is this an advantage?
3. Second, he had big hands, large feet, and long limbs.	Why were these advantages?
4. These physical advantages gave him confidence.	How?
5. It is not surprising that he was the best swimmer in his hometown.	Why?

sentence	question
1. Traveling is not only a good way for people to relax and escape the pressure of daily routines, it is also very educational.	How is it educational?
2. Traveling teaches people a lot about other cultures.	What does it teach?
3. Visiting other places can also improve communication skills.	How?
4. Finally, traveling can make a person interested in studying at a college or university.	How?
5. Traveling is a good way to learn.	Why?

Finally, read how the paragraphs have been developed to answer specific questions. The new information is underlined. Besides being better developed, the new paragraphs are more interesting.

A. Lee was the most successful swimmer in his hometown because he had many physical advantages. First, he was taller than most of his competitors. Whereas the average height of most male swimmers was 5′10″, Lee was 6′1 1/2″ tall. This gave him an advantage during starts and turns in races. Second, he had big hands, large feet, and long limbs that allowed him to catch and hold more water than other swimmers, giving more propulsion than others in the same number of strokes. These physical advantages gave him confidence and with this confidence he worked hard and improved his strokes. With his physical advantages and positive attitude, he won many swim meets. It is not surprising he was the best swimmer in his hometown.

B. Traveling is not only a good way for people to relax and escape the pressure of daily routines, but it is also very educational. Many travelers return home with more than just memories of a good time; they come home with more knowledge and broader horizons. Traveling teaches people a lot about other cultures. In another culture, a person can explore the traditions and values of a people by observing their customs and making friends. Visiting other places can also improve communication skills. Meeting people from different countries encourages the tourist to learn new languages and to try to build friendships. Finally, traveling can make a person interested in studying at a college or university. After visiting historical monuments, art museums, and so on and after struggling with new languages, a traveler may be interested in history, art, or linguistics and may return to college. Indeed, traveling is a good way to learn.

focus on testing

Outlining Ideas

When writing under time pressure, as in a placement or exit exam, it is a good idea to jot down your ideas in the form of an outline before you begin writing. This will help you organize your thoughts, clarify your general ideas, and check to see that you have included enough specific details in your essay.

Practicing What You've Learned

The following paragraphs are not well developed. Each sentence in the paragraphs is followed by a question. Rewrite and develop the paragraphs by providing your own answers to the questions. Of course, your answers will be based on your own opinions and experiences. You can change words and/or phrases in the original version to make your paragraph better.

A. My favorite vacation was the one I took several years ago. (Where? When? Why?) I met some nice people and saw some interesting sights. (Who? What? How?) I'll never forget that vacation. (Why?) I hope I have another one like it soon.

B. Whenever my friend Sharon, a film student, has extra time and money, she goes to the movies. She particularly likes international films. (Why?) She has learned a lot about Asian and European film directors. (How? So what?) Her class on filmmaking has also taught her a lot. (So what?) If Sharon weren't a student with so much to do, she would spend all her time in movie theaters.

C. Skateboarding is the least appealing sport I know. (Why?) Only agile young people can do it. (So what?) It is dangerous not only for the riders, but also for the innocent pedestrians who get swept off their feet on the sidewalk. (How?) Skateboarders wear strange clothes and even stranger hairstyles. (Why?) Who ever invented skateboarding?

Develop the following superficial paragraphs by *asking* and *answering* questions at the end of each sentence. Refer to Part One of this chapter and your own knowledge and experience to add supporting examples. Exchange papers with a classmate when you are finished.

A. Watching television has both advantages and disadvantages. It provides entertainment. It may also be informative or educational. On the other hand, it is a passive activity. It may take us away from other things we should be doing. There are both positive and negative aspects of television.

B. Soccer is the most popular sport in many countries. People have played it for a long time. Good soccer players require physical stamina. They must practice long and hard to learn to control the ball with their feet. It is a difficult game to play and an exciting sport to watch.

C. Many people like to collect things as a hobby. A lifetime of gathering can result in some very impressive collections. While stamp collecting and coin collecting are well-known examples, there are other objects that are less common as collectors' items. These are dolls, plates, crystal figurines, teacups, painted eggshells, and baby spoons. Almost anything can be a collector's item.

Writing Assignments

Write an essay about one of the following topics. Use new vocabulary and expressions you learned in this chapter and make sure that your paragraphs are clear and coherent. Develop your ideas by using information from the research you did in Part One.

1. Describe the ways in which students at your school spend their leisure time.
2. Write about one or more of the activities you learned about in your interview in Part One.
3. Discuss the advantages and disadvantages of the Olympic Games. Consider politics, international cooperation, and athletic excellence.
4. Write about your favorite sport or a popular sport in your country. Include in your essay some background on the sport and what physical (and psychological) strengths are necessary for players to succeed.

5. Write about any aspect of leisure-time activities that interests you.

PART four

Evaluating for Rewriting

Working with Your Partner

Number the sentences in each of the paragraphs of the body of your essay. (You don't need to do this for the introduction.) Begin again with (1) for each paragraph. Then exchange papers with your classmate, and answer the following questions about his or her essay.

1. After reading the introduction and thesis, what kinds of questions do you expect the writer to answer?

   ____

   ____

2. Read each paragraph. Has the writer developed the ideas adequately? That is, were you, as the reader, left with any questions about the main idea of the paragraph? If your answer is *yes,* write the number(s) of the sentence(s) and the questions it doesn't answer. Do this for each paragraph.

PARAGRAPH 1

Sentence Number Questions to Be Answered

____

____

____

PARAGRAPH 2

Sentence Number Questions to Be Answered

____

____

____

PARAGRAPH 3

Sentence Number Questions to Be Answered

____

____

____

3. Now look at how the ideas are linked to each other. Is there a smooth connection from sentence to sentence? If you think the writer could improve the coherence, indicate the paragraph and sentence numbers for improvement.

____

____

4. Do you have any further general recommendations for the writer of this essay?

____

____

5. Can you find any mistakes in the writer's use of countable or uncountable nouns? If you're not sure, write the nouns in question below and the writer will review Part Two to make sure he or she hasn't made a mistake.

____

____

____

Return each other's essays. Read your partner's evaluation of your essay. Discuss any questions you have with your partner.

Working on Your Own

After evaluating your partner's essay, you should be ready to evaluate your own work with some objectivity. Go through the questions again. Take into consideration what your partner said about your essay when he or she evaluated it. Is there more to add? Are there words to change? Can you clear up any language mistakes?

Rewrite your essay, making any necessary changes. Turn this revised draft of your essay in to your teacher.

CHAPTER **eight**

Creativity

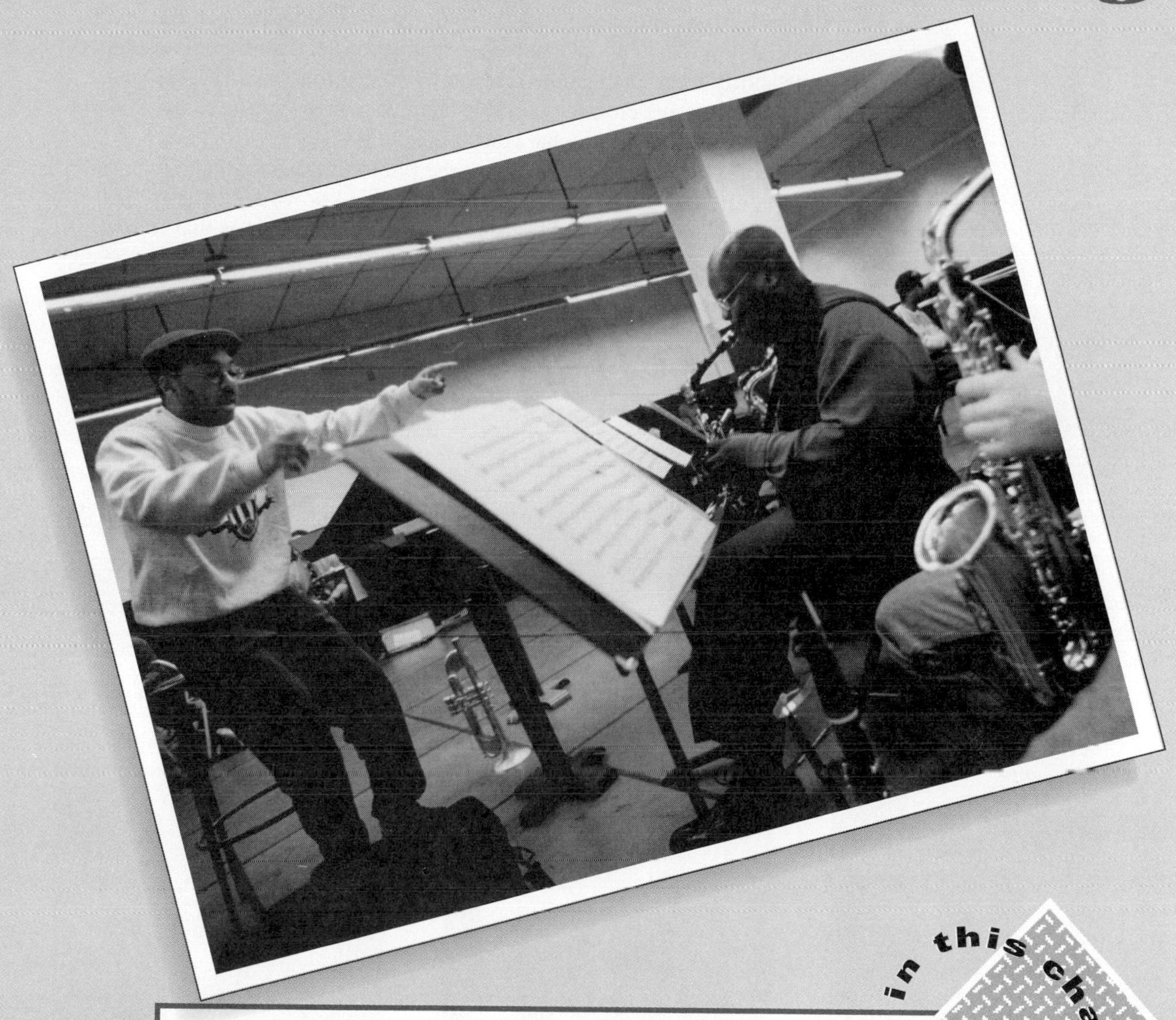

in this chapter

You will research information about a creative person and write about an aspect of creativity that interests you.

PART one
Ideas for Writing

Getting Started

We often think of artists and writers when we think of creative people, but inventors, scientists, and business people also use creative skills. Creativity is usually defined as the ability to produce something new and original, so almost any human activity can involve creativity. In this chapter, you are going to think about where creativity comes from and what contributes to it.

Look at the following photos (along with the photo of musician, conductor, and composer Wynton Marsalis on page 149) of people known for their creative efforts. Study the photos and, in small groups, answer the questions that follow.

1. Isabel Allende, writer

2. Joan Chen, actress

3. Wayne Wang, film maker

4. Alicia Alonso, dancer/choreographer

5. Helen Frankenthaler, artist

6. Luis Valdez, writer/director

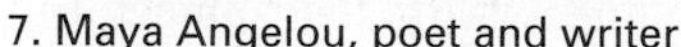

7. Maya Angelou, poet and writer

8. Steve Jobs, founder of Apple Computer

1. Discuss each of the photos. Do you recognize any of these people? Share what you know about them with your partners.
2. Describe what each person appears to be doing.
3. What do these people have in common that makes them *creative*?
4. Now think about other creative people who may or may not be famous. Why are *they* creative?

Brainstorming

The pictures on these pages show various people involved in creative activities. What do you think inspires them? Where do artists get their ideas? With two or three other classmates, make a list of all the possible things that could contribute to an artist's (or anyone's) creativity. Begin with the pictures you just looked at.

Freewriting

Do you consider yourself to be a creative person? What creative activities do you do? Where and when do you feel the most creative? What inspires you to be creative? Write for fifteen minutes without stopping about creativity and you.

Reading for Ideas

The following passage is adapted from an article by Bill Moyers, a journalist and producer of wide experience who is best known for his TV documentaries. In this selection, Moyers describes what he found to be the meaning of creativity during the production of a recent documentary on that subject. Before you read, answer the following questions.

prereading questions

1. The title of the following selection is *Defining Creativity for Everyone to See Wasn't Exactly Easy.* First, why do you think it is difficult to define creativity for everyone? Second, what are some different ways to define creativity?

   ____

   ____

   ____

2. In his article, Moyers refers to Bernard Malamud, George Prince, and Maya Angelou. What do you know about them?

   ____

   ____

   ____

3. Have you seen any of Moyers' programs? Describe what you watched and your impressions.

   ____

   ____

   ____

4. In your opinion, where does creativity come from? Are certain people born with creativity, or can anyone learn it? Is it possible that both of these conditions are true?

   ____

   ____

   ____

   ____

Defining Creativity for Everyone to See Wasn't Exactly Easy

It all started innocently enough. I had set out to learn what I could about creativity. And there I was: an amateur with a cause and three colleagues: two people from the Corporation for Entertainment and Learning, and my wife and coeditor, Judith, who is an educational consultant—all tossed about on a turbulent sea churned by the high-horsepower engines of scientists, scholars, psychiatrists, historians, educators, sociologists and philosophers whose careers have been devoted to exploring creativity.

The waves came over our little boat almost immediately. Here was the very considerable novelist Bernard Malamud declaring that "creativity is a complex thing . . . Maybe sometime in the future they actually will find the genetic tissue that makes it what it is. I don't want to be around when that happens. I want artistic creativity to remain forever a mystery."

On the other hand, there was the author George Prince acknowledging that although once he had thought of creativity as an extraordinary act of producing something new and useful, now he sees it "as less cosmic and more common, an everyday affair, a mode of thought and action that is ultimately associated with learning and changing not only one's self but one's situation."

There you have it—the basic tension between those who believe creativity to be a mystery, possibly a gift to genius alone, and those who believe it can be demystified, nurtured, even democratized. One school will have nothing to do with trying to dissect creativity into scientifically defined variables. Another considers creativity to be the endowment of all of us. Actually, the conflict represents not only opposing views of creativity but also differing ideas about human nature.

Two things are implied in the word "creativity," as I have come to understand it: novelty and significance. What is created is new, and the new opens up paths that expand human possibilities. All creative behavior breaks from the past but remains indebted to it. Maya Angelou—poet, author, director, actress—told me that she never "left" Stamps, Arkansas, although she had moved from the little Southwest Arkansas town 30 years ago: "You carry your home wherever you go." When I asked Maya Angelou to go back with me to where her own nascent creativity was first threatened and then forged, she did not want to go. But finally she agreed, and we glimpsed just how creative behavior grows from deep roots, which it never totally severs even as it transcends them.

There are other examples. Fred Smith, who founded Federal Express, had some compelling sense of duty which motivated him from childhood and became obsessive while he was in Vietnam. Samson Raphaelson, the playwright, says that the drive to be creative has its roots in some remote past no longer operating consciously but still there nonetheless. The inventions we shall see are all examples of departures from tradition, but none could have occurred without tradition.

Creative people, then, often look at something from the past that is the result of convergent thinking, and by thinking about it divergently, come up with a novel use of a familiar object. They look in the commonplace to find the strange. Instead of thinking toward old solutions, they think away from them, making the leap from the unexpected to the inspired. Poets do it with metaphors and similes. Journalists can do it with garbage. Yes, garbage. It was the first subject we decided to explore because we sensed that it would be a useful vehicle for demonstrating that you can think creatively about almost anything, if you learn how to relate and connect what at casual glance seems odd to couple. In our research we found an Arizona professor, a garbologist, teaching contemporary civilization through what people throw out; a New York artist turning ordinary things off the streets into works of art; and an East Texas sewage plant where earthworms are used to turn sludge into topsoil.

We realized early in our reporting that there may be as many creative processes as there are creative people. And we decided that any full picturing of creativity would require many images. However, the people I met did confirm a number of characteristics about the nature of creative behavior. Creative people tolerate ambiguity. They have an unremitting desire to create a satisfying new order out of chaos, and the courage to persist to create that order on one's own terms. This makes them often cantankerous, sometimes exasperating, always unconventional. What matters to them is not what others think of them but what they think of themselves.

Bill Moyers

postreading questions

1. What are the two opposing views about creativity?

____

____

2. Record the different people's definitions of creativity in the following chart. Try to summarize their opinions in your own words. Then add your own definition.

What Is Creativity?

according to	Bernard Malamud	George Prince	Maya Angelou	Bill Moyers	you
Who is she or he?					
What's her or his definition?					

3. Why did Moyers' team choose to explore garbage?

____

____

4. Tell your classmates about some people whom you consider to be creative in your current community. Would Moyers agree with you that these people are creative?

____

____

____

____

THINKING CRITICALLY

Analyzing Metaphors

A *metaphor* is a word or expression that a speaker or a writer uses to suggest something different from the word or expression's literal meaning. For example, Bill Moyers uses a metaphor in the third sentence of his essay on creativity. He states that he and his colleagues were ". . . all tossed about on a turbulent sea. . . ." In fact, he and his colleagues weren't literally tossing about on a turbulent sea; rather, he uses the metaphor to show how confused they felt as they were exploring a complex issue.

In his essay, Moyers includes a quote from Maya Angelou, which contains another metaphor: "You carry your home wherever you go." In small groups, analyze Maya Angelou's metaphor. What does she mean by this statement? After you analyze her metaphor, discuss how true or untrue the statement is for you personally.

Gathering Information

Research one of the people in the pictures on pages 149 to 151 or a creative person of your choice. Look for information like Moyers did that explores why and how this person is creative. Organize your information in an outline like the one that follows. Give a brief presentation of the results of your research to your classmates. Include the points in the following outline.

I. Background about the creative person
- **A.** What is the creative person's best-known work?
- **B.** When and where did she or he live?
- **C.** Which individuals inspired/influenced/pushed this person?
- **D.** What are/were the creative person's special skills or talents?

II. The creative person's process
- **A.** Does/did the creative person work in a special place?
- **B.** Does/did the creative person use special tools or materials?
- **C.** Does/did the creative person have special rituals during the creative process?

III. How does this person's creativity relate to one of the definitions presented in the Moyers article?

PART two
Language for Writing

Making Comparisons

In the previous section, you learned about the creative process of different people. When comparing two people or two things, you discuss either their *similarities* or their *differences* (and sometimes both). Special expressions are used to describe similarities and differences clearly to the reader.

Here is a list of some of the most important expressions for making comparisons. Study the different ways of comparing X and Y.

SIMILARITIES

X is as (adjective) as Y.

Both X and Y are. . . .

DIFFERENCES

X is . . . , but Y is. . . .

$X \text{ is } \left\{ \begin{array}{l} \text{(adjective)} + \textit{er} \\ \text{more + (adjective)} \end{array} \right\} \text{ than } Y$

X is less (adjective) than Y.

SIMILARITIES	DIFFERENCES
Neither X nor Y is. . .	X and Y are different.
X can be compared to Y.	X and Y are different in that. . . .
X and Y are alike in that they share (certain) charactcristics. . . .	X differs from Y in that (because). . . .
X has something in common with Y.	Unlike X, Y is. . . .
X is similar to (like) Y.	Although / Even though / Whereas } X is. . . , Y is. . . .
X is similar to Y in that. . . .	X is. . . . On the other hand, Y is. . . .
Like X, Y is. . . .	

Study the following examples, noting punctuation. Underline the comparison expressions.

1. Both Gertrude Stein and Ernest Hemingway were innovative American authors who expressed their ideas in short, simple sentences.
2. Unlike many other writers, the Korean novelist LeHuang Su moved from the city to the country to write about life in an urban area.
3. Picasso was similar to other notable artists in that his extraordinary talent was recognized when he was a young boy.

Describing the Creative Process

The following words and expressions from Moyers' essay are useful for writing about creativity and creative people. Find them in their original contexts in the essay and underline them.

NOUNS	ADJECTIVES	EXPRESSIONS
mystery	nascent	artistic creativity
genius	cantankerous	to expand human possibilities
novelty	exasperating	creative behavior
significance	unconventional	a sense of duty
endowment		the drive to be creative
		convergent/divergent thinking
		creative processes
		to tolerate ambiguity
		to create order out of chaos

Now, to make sure you understand what each one means, use these words and expressions to describe people you know to a partner.

Practicing What You've Learned

Study the expressions on page 157 for making comparisons (paying attention to punctuation as well as sentence structure). Then correct the mistakes in the following sentences. There is one mistake in each sentence.

1. Like Mozart Beethoven had a father who pushed him in his early years.
2. Although Henry Moore and Geoffrey Chaucer were different kinds of artists and lived at different times they were both inspired and influenced by great artists of the past.
3. Neither LeHuang Su nor John Steinbeck were interested in writing about life in the big city.

Write about the people in the photos in Part One or other artists of your choice. Use material you gathered from Part One or information you learned from your classmates' presentations. Use ten different expressions from the list of comparisons in this section. Then exchange your sentences with a partner.

Rewrite your Freewriting exercise from page 152 using some of the words and expression from the lists in Describing the Creative Process.

Write a paragraph about the person you researched for Gathering Information on page 156. Use some of the words and expressions from the lists in Describing the Creative Process.

PART three
Systems for Writing

Paragraph Coherence

Review Points

- You can make paragraphs coherent by repeating key words and phrases throughout the paragraph.
- You can also achieve coherence by paraphrasing key words and phrases as you develop your ideas in the paragraph.

Listing Signals

> **New Points**
> - *Listing signals* are words that give order to ideas and link ideas in one sentence to those in another; they can make a paragraph coherent.
> - You can use listing signals to describe events that have a chronological order.
> - You can also use them to list points that support your topic sentence, even if the points don't have a chronological relationship.

Study these listing signals. Then read the paragraphs to see how they are used.

LISTING SIGNALS			
	First,	Next,	Last,
	Second,	Then,	Finally,
	Third,	Later,	

A. I follow a strict routine whenever I get ready to write. First, I get my favorite pen out and I sharpen all my pencils. Next, I clear my desk and pull out my tablet of yellow paper. Then, I fix myself a cup of hot tea and set it on a coaster on my desk. Finally, I turn on the radio to my favorite classical music station and close the door. Following these steps makes it easier for me to concentrate on my ideas whenever I have writing to do.

B. David's work is different from the work of most artists. First, his pieces are very large and cannot be displayed in small studios. They need big walls and spacious rooms. Second, his art is abstract, combining a variety of techniques: painting, plastering, sanding, scraping, molding, and spraying. Finally, the pieces themselves are very unusual. They present odd forms and beautiful colors. The work of this artist is a dramatic departure from conventional painting.

Sentence Connectors

> **New Points**
> - You can also establish paragraph coherence by using *sentence connectors.*
> - Sentence connectors show relationships between ideas in different sentences in a paragraph.
> - Sentence connectors link independent clauses and usually come between two sentences. However, if the sentences are short, connectors come after a semicolon (;).
> - Do not use too many sentence connectors (and listing signals) because this will make your writing repetitive.

Take a look at these examples:

1. Marcel Proust could write only in bed; similarly, Hemingway had to do his work in a special place.
2. Some people require peace and quiet in order to write. However, others need the stimulation and excitement of public places.

Study these sentence connectors. Then read the paragraphs and answer the questions that follow.

sentence connectors	functions	examples
Similarly, Likewise, In the same way, (These expressions indicate similarities.) In addition, Furthermore, Moreover, Besides,	Introduce a new/additional idea that supports the previous sentence	Creative writing is a means of communication; *furthermore,* it helps people understand their own feelings.
However, On the other hand, Conversely, In contrast,	Show the other side, a contrasting point, or differences	Filmmaking requires a lot of resources, such as money and equipment. *However,* writing poetry only requires paper and pencil.
For example, In fact,	Expand a point by providing a specific illustration or application	Carol Evans is a prolific filmmaker. *In fact,* she produced eight documentaries last year.
Thus, Therefore, In conclusion,	Conclude a point by providing a result; may relate to two or three previous sentences	People become better writers through the act of writing; *therefore,* if you want to get published, you should write every day.

A. Both writing and pottery making are crafts that require special skills. The apprentice writer and potter are alike because they learn their skills through instruction and practice. The best instruction comes from studying a master, someone skilled in the craft. The potter must begin by observing the master, then working with the clay himself or herself. The writer begins by reading good writing and by identifying the characteristics that make it good. The potter begins with small projects and then, after gaining skill and confidence, takes on larger projects. The writer starts with short paragraphs before attempting essays. Only after a great deal of practice and careful imitation of master craftsmen can a potter form an object of beauty. Only after writing, rewriting, and studying model works can a writer turn out a successful essay.

B. Writers and potters are similar in that they both learn their crafts by imitating masters, people skilled in the craft. They devote a great deal of time and concentration to following these masters. For example, before the potter can produce a delicate vase or a symmetrical pitcher, he or she must spend time watching a master at work. Likewise, a novice writer cannot produce a well-organized essay or even a coherent paragraph without first studying good models. The potter observes the way the expert spins the wheel and forms the clay; then he or she tries to do exactly what the master has done. Similarly, the apprentice writer imitates the work of a master writer. The potter begins with small, simple projects. In the same way, the writer begins with short paragraphs and proceeds to the essay only after mastering the basics. So just as the potter gains inspiration and skill from an experienced artist, a writer learns to communicate effectively after studying the work of master writers.

1. Which paragraph did you find easier to read? Can you determine why?

____

____

2. The smoother paragraph (the second one) has sentences that are linked together by sentence connectors. Go back and underline as many sentence connectors as you can find.

Organizing A Comparison Paragraph

Review Point

One way to organize a paragraph is to start with a topic sentence, then present examples that support it, and conclude with a restatement of the topic sentence.

New Points

- When you write a paragraph that compares people or things, you usually focus on similarities or differences.
- One way to write a topic sentence for a comparison paragraph is to state that X and Y are similar or different, and tell how or why they are similar or different.

  example: A writer and a potter are similar in that each learns a craft by imitating an expert.

Here are two ways to organize a comparison paragraph:

1. The first way is to list all the points about X and then all the points about Y. Your paragraph looks like this:

   Topic sentence.

   XXXXXXXXXXXXXXXXXXXXXXXXXXXXXXXXXXXXXXXX
   XXXXXXXXXXXXXXXXXXXXXXXXXXXXXXXXXXXXXXXX
   On the other hand, YYYYYYYYYYYYYYYYYYYYYYYYYYYYYYY
   YYYYYYYYYYYYYYYYYYYYYYYYYYYYYYYYYYYYYYYYY
   YYYYYYYYYYYYYYYYYYYYYYYYYYYYYYYYYYYYYYYYY

2. The second way is to describe X and Y for each point of difference or similarity. In this case, the paragraph looks like this:

   Topic sentence.

   XXXXXXX YYYYYYY XXXXXXX YYYYYYY XXXXXXX
   YYYYYYY XXXXXXX YYYYYYY XXXXXX YYYYYY

Practicing What You've Learned

In the following paragraph, the writer has mistakenly used too many listing signals and sentence connectors. With your classmates, rewrite the paragraph by eliminating some of the listing signals so that the sentences are more varied and interesting.

Wayne Wang, the Chinese-American film director who became a surprising success story in 1982 with *Chan Is Missing*, always knew that he would succeed in film in America. First, his father named him after the American actor John Wayne. Second, he grew up loving American films and idolizing movie stars. Third, he came to the United States for college. Then, he got his master's degree in film. Finally, he was introduced to experimental films that prompted him to break the stereotype of Asians in the movies. Now, Wang is a successful filmmaker whose work—such as the highly acclaimed *Joy Luck Club*—deals with the complexities of being Asian in America.

Read the following paragraphs. Which pattern of organization discussed on the top of page 162 does each paragraph follow?

A. Writing an essay in Japanese is not as difficult as writing an essay in English because the writing rules are not as strict. Unlike an essay in English, a Japanese essay doesn't have to stick to the topic or have a thesis statement. In English, the ideas should be clearly stated and developed. In Japanese, however, it is acceptable to write vague, subtle, and even ambiguous sentences. In an English essay, the conclusion is in the final part of the paragraph or essay. In contrast, the conclusion in a Japanese essay can appear at the beginning or the end of the essay, depending on the style. Whereas a Japanese writer can include two or three main ideas in a paragraph, an English writer must limit the paragraph to one. Because the rules are not as strict, it is easier to write an essay in Japanese than in English. *—Rica Kuno*

B. Writing letters is more enjoyable than writing compositions. It is fun to write letters to friends and family, as one doesn't have to worry about topic sentences, supporting sentences, or mistakes in grammar. The writer can write about many topics and include as many paragraphs as he or she wants. There is no time limit to writing a letter, so it can be done whenever the writer is in the mood. On the other hand, writing a composition is not as much fun. Each paragraph must begin with a topic sentence and continue with sentences that support it. The writer has to be careful to correct mistakes in grammar and include a paragraph for each supporting idea in the thesis statement. The time for writing a composition is usually restricted, so the writer cannot put it off until he or she feels like doing it. Because of all these rules, writing a composition is much less enjoyable than writing a letter. *—Rafael Garcia*

With a partner, choose two artists from Part One and compare or contrast them. Both of you should write about the same things (either similarities or differences) but organize your paragraphs differently. When you have finished, exchange paragraphs and discuss which pattern of organization was the best suited to the topic.

Improve the paragraph on the next page by combining sentences or adding listing signals or sentence connectors. Compare your work with your classmates when you are finished.

Steven Spielberg is unequivocally one of the world's most famous and successful filmmakers. *Jurassic Park* earned more money than any other movie in history. The video of *Jurassic Park* will continue to earn even more money. Two of Spielberg's other famous films, *E.T.: The Extra-Terrestrial* and *Jaws*, also set record earnings at the box office. His action-adventure films, *Raiders of the Lost Ark* and *Indiana Jones and the Temple of Doom*, were also blockbuster hits. Both films starred actor Harrison Ford. The moving drama, *Schindler's List*, was another victory for Spielberg. *Schindler's List* won the Academy Award for Best Picture in 1994. The name Steven Spielberg is well-known the world over; his movies are even more famous.

exercise 5 Rewrite a paragraph from a previous assignment. Make it more coherent and interesting by adding listing signals or sentence connectors.

exercise 6 Write a paragraph about the *process* an artist follows when producing a piece of art. Choose the artist you researched in Part One and make your paragraph coherent by using listing signals.

In Part Three, Chapter Five, you learned about three types of introductions: general-to-specific, problem-solution, and chronological. Take a chronological introduction from one of your past essays and rewrite it using some of the listing signals you studied in this section.

focus on testing

Avoiding Repetition

Exercise 1 on page 162 asked you to edit a paragraph for overuse of listing signals and sentence connectors. Whenever you have to write an essay on a standardized test, edit your writing for overuse of these sentence coherence devices. This will make your writing more fluent and sophisticated.

Writing Assignments

Write an essay on one of the following topics. Use new vocabulary and expressions you learned in this chapter; make sure that your paragraphs are clear and coherent. Develop your ideas by using information from your research in Part One.

1. Think of two people famous for their creativity. They can be artists, scientists, businesspeople, etc. Choose one aspect of their lives or work and compare them. You might choose to discuss how they are (were) inspired, their workstyles, their writing styles, their subjects, their habits, their lifestyles, or their philosophies.
2. The following quotations, one from a painter and the other from a writer, make similar statements about what takes place during the creative process. Study the quotes to determine what they mean. Then choose one of them and compare this approach to creativity with a different approach you have learned about in this chapter.

   "The picture is not thought out and determined beforehand: rather while it is being made it follows the mobility of thought." —*Pablo Picasso*

   "Think of writing, then, not as a way to transmit a message but as a way to grow and cook a message." —*Peter Elbow*

3. Write an essay in which you examine the similarities and/or differences between two of the following creative activities, or any two activities of your choice:

writing a song	painting a picture	building a house
writing a poem	sculpting	filmmaking
writing an essay	cooking	designing clothes

4. Many famous artists attribute their success to their teachers or masters. Read the following quotation by Leonardo da Vinci, and then write about the influence of an artist's master on his or her work.

> "Poor is the student who doesn't surpass his master." —*Leonardo da Vinci*

5. After having completed this chapter and after having read many opinions on the definition of creativity, write an essay explaining your personal definition of creativity. Use specific examples of creative people and creative processes to support your opinion.

free choice

6. Write about any aspect of creativity that interests you.

PART four

Evaluating for Rewriting

Working with Your Partner

step 1

Exchange the essays you wrote for the Writing Assignments section. Use the following questionnaire to evaluate each other's essays.

1. Read the essay to get a general impression (don't focus on details). What is your impression after one reading?
   a. It's clear—I like it.
   b. I understand what the writer wants to say, but some parts are unclear.
   c. The essay needs to be developed further.

2. Look at the specific features. Find the thesis. Write it here.

   ____

   ____

3. Look at the topic sentences in the paragraphs of the body. Do they directly support the thesis? If not, how could they be improved?

   Topic Sentence 1 yes no ______________________

   Topic Sentence 2 yes no ______________________

   Topic Sentence 3 yes no ______________________

4. Read the body paragraphs. Rate the following features by circling + or –. Give the writer specific suggestions when possible.

	UNITY	ORGANIZATION	COHERENCE	SPECIFIC DETAILS
Paragraph 1:	+ –	+ –	+ –	+ –
Paragraph 2:	+ –	+ –	+ –	+ –
Paragraph 3:	+ –	+ –	+ –	+ –

5. Which organizational pattern does the writer use? ____________________

   Is it effective?

   Yes _____ No _____

6. Choose one of the paragraphs of the body. How many sentence connectors does the writer use? _____

   Should the writer change some of the sentence connectors?

   Yes _____ No _____

   Should the writer add some sentence connectors?

   Yes _____ No _____

   Should the writer omit some sentence connectors?

   Yes _____ No _____

   Specify the changes the writer should make.

   ____

   ____

   ____

7. How many examples of similarities or differences does the writer use in the essay? _____ What are they?

   ____

   ____

   ____

   Should the writer add more? Yes _____ No _____

8. Do you have any further specific comments to help the writer improve the essay? Write them here:

   ____

   ____

step 2

Return each other's essays. Read your partner's evaluation of your essay. Discuss any questions you have with your partner.

Working on Your Own

Now you should be ready to evaluate your own essay. Go through the questions again. Take into consideration what your partner said about your essay when he or she evaluated it. Is there more to add? Words to change?

Rewrite your essay, making any necessary changes. Turn this revised draft of your essay in to your teacher.

CHAPTER nine

Human Behavior

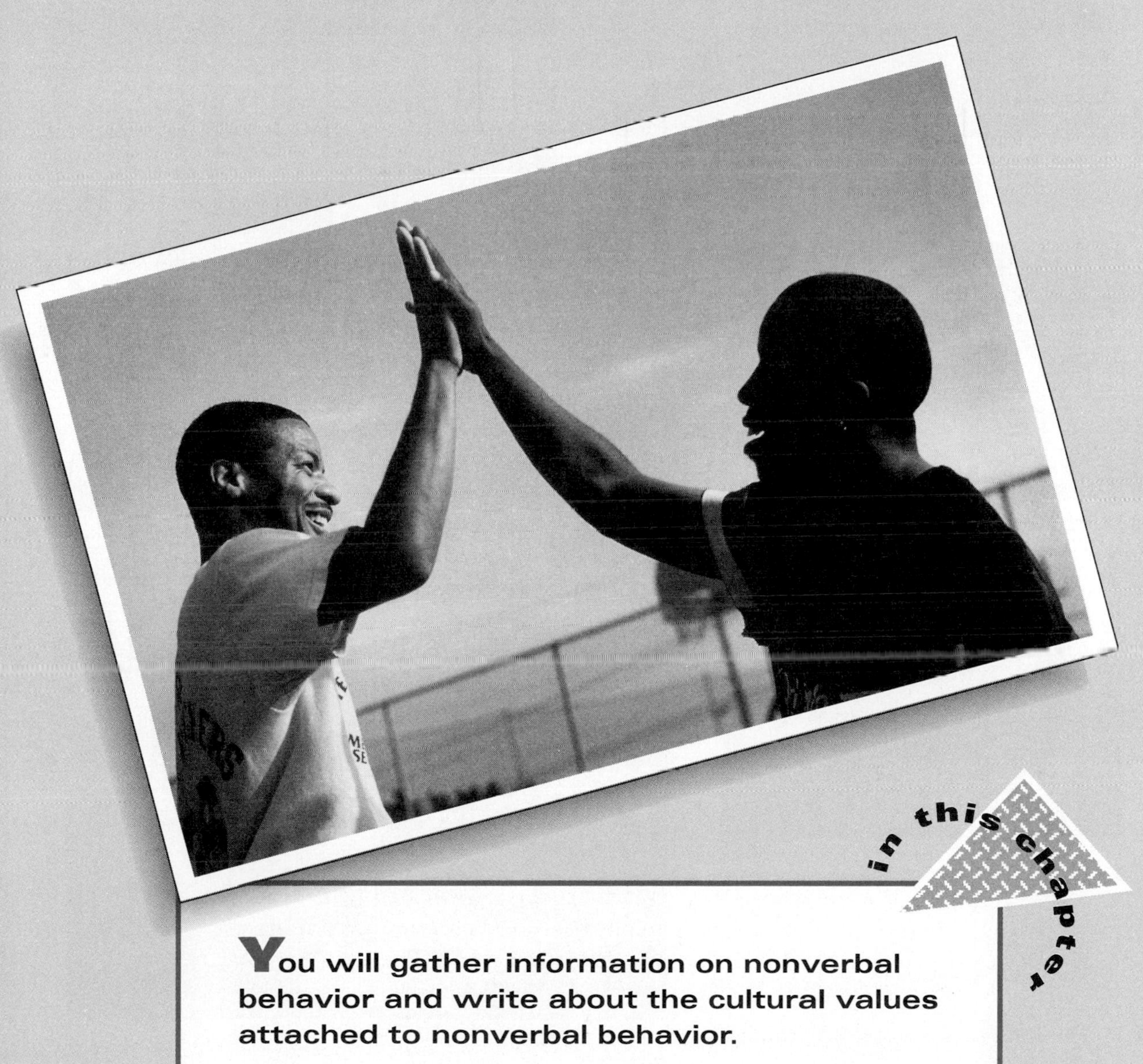

in this chapter

You will gather information on nonverbal behavior and write about the cultural values attached to nonverbal behavior.

1.

2.

3.

4.

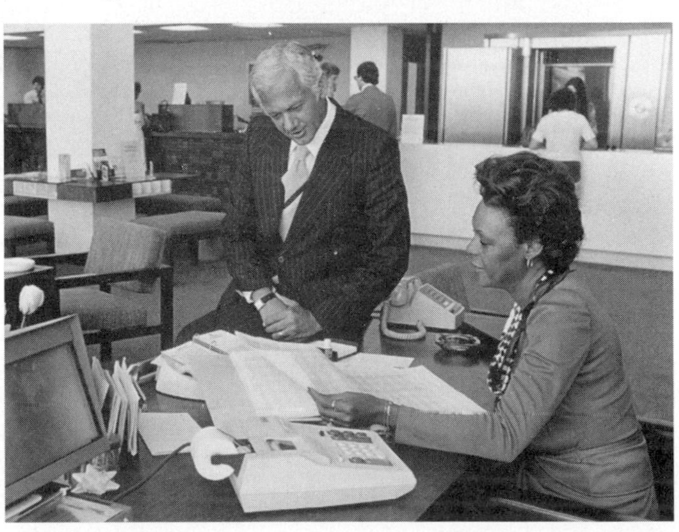

5.

Ideas for Writing

Getting Started

Have you ever noticed the way some people communicate with their hands and other parts of their body? How much information do you think people can communicate without language?

The photographs on the facing page show people from different countries and culture's communicating without words. What are they "saying?" Where are they from? Discuss the answers to these questions with a classmate.

Brainstorming

With a partner from your home country or alone, use the following chart to make a list of some common ways you communicate without words. Then share your information with the class.

nonverbal behavior in ______________________
(country)

What do you do?	*What does it mean?*
______________	______________
______________	______________
______________	______________
______________	______________
______________	______________
______________	______________

Freewriting

Think of one example of nonverbal behavior in your country that has a different interpretation in the United States or Canada. Think about facial expressions, gestures, or how people use time or space. Write for fifteen minutes about this behavior and how it might lead to a cross-cultural misunderstanding in another country. The hand gesture in the picture on the next page is an example. In Japan, it means "come here," but in the United States it means "go away."

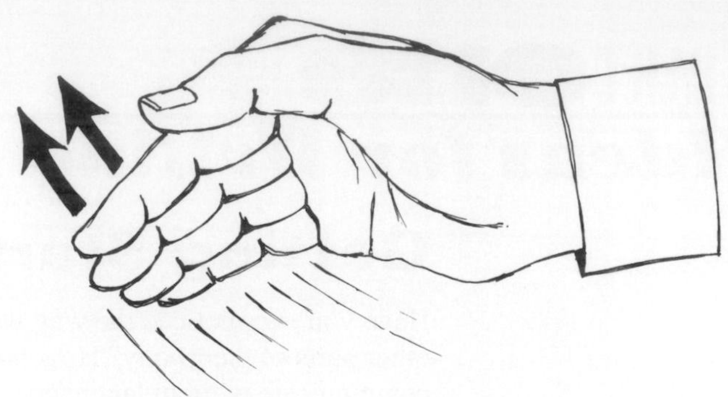

Reading for Ideas

The following selection is an excerpt from an article by Fathi Yousef. Professor Yousef is a specialist in the cross-cultural aspects of nonverbal communication. He teaches in the Speech Department at California State University in Long Beach, California.

prereading questions

1. The following article describes some misunderstandings resulting from nonverbal behavior. First, share with your classmates an example of a cross-cultural misunderstanding. Then read the following situation. What cross-cultural misunderstanding might arise? Write your prediction on the lines.

   An American customer is waiting to be helped in a busy department store in Puerto Rico or in a Greek grocery store in San Francisco.

   ____

   ____

   ____

   ____

2. After you read the selection, go back to your prediction. Was it accurate?

Nonverbal Behavior: Some Intricate and Diverse Dimensions in Intercultural Communication

John Smith has just returned to New York from a vacation in Puerto Rico. John told his friends that since he understood and spoke Spanish, he had no problems communicating with people over there. John also said that he wasn't surprised that the area was not well developed economically. "After all, people there have no sense of organization. Even their business behavior is quite disorganized," John said. "For instance, I once walked to a counter in one of the largest department stores in San Juan, the capital, around noon. The salesman was talking to a couple of native customers; however, as soon as I arrived, he greeted me and asked what he could do for me. I thanked him and told him to attend first to those he was already serving. The salesman smiled and continued the transaction with his customers. In the meantime, other people arrived, interrupted, were served, and left while I stood quietly fuming and waiting for my turn, which, incidentally, the salesman never acknowledged. I tell you these people don't have any sense of order or business."

In this example there is a communication breakdown based primarily on misunderstanding and unawareness of the subtle cultural nonverbal cues. John Smith, in Puerto Rico, though able to speak Spanish, when faced with a different concept of time reverted to his own cultural behavior patterns and found Puerto Ricans having no sense of order or business. John Smith, in that department store, misunderstood the interactional cycle of behavior in terms of the culture's perception of time. John Smith expected a monochronic pattern of interpersonal communication, where one customer at a time was attended to, and every customer was to be served in the order of his arrival. What happened was that John Smith was faced with a polychronic concept of time, where the salesman did not serve one customer at a time but rather tried to serve all customers at the same time. John Smith acted and reacted according to his North American cultural expectations: Time is structured in monochronic segments. Things are attended to one at a time. In this instance, customers should expect to be served in the order of their arrival or they are owed an apology or an explanation. Or, to be charitable, it is simply an inefficient and failing organization. On the other hand, from the salesman's cultural perspective he felt he had done his duty and was quite courteous. As soon as John Smith walked in, he was greeted and his presence was acknowledged while the transactions with other customers were continuing efficiently. John Smith, however, was quiet and seemed to want to wait, or maybe he wanted to look around for a while before he made up his mind. Anyway, he never mentioned what he wanted while many other customers arrived, were served, and left.

The salesman's behavior reflects a polychronic segmentation of time in interpersonal relations where interaction at several different levels is carried on simultaneously. The same behavior can be observed here for example, in Any Town, U.S.A., in ethnic Armenian, Greek, Lebanese, or Syrian grocery stores where we see the "foreign" salesperson trying to serve several customers simultaneously and regardless of the order of their arrival. In social or business interactions involving a North American and a Latin American or a Middle Easterner, or sometimes certain Southern Europeans, the North American may be talking or listening to the other party when the "foreigner" may "interrupt inappropriately" to acknowledge the presence of another individual. In no case is either party's business or social behavior inefficient, slighting, or insulting, or intended to frustrate, irritate, or aggravate. It is simply a different cultural structuring and meaning of temporal cycles in interpersonal interactions.

Fathi Yousef

postreading questions

1. In a brief summary, describe what happened in the San Juan department store in the article. Write as if you were an objective observer, noticing only the actions that took place but not interpreting them. Arrange your report in a chronological list.

a. ______________________________

b. ______________________________

c. ______________________________

d. ______________________________

e. ______________________________

f. ______________________________

2. John Smith describes his experience in a department store in San Juan in the first paragraph. Pretend you are the salesman. How would you describe the incident with John Smith?

____

____

____

____

____

____

3. The following diagrams are referred to as "open minds." They are used to represent a person's thoughts and feelings. Fill in the open minds with pictures words, phrases or sentences that represent the thoughts and/or feelings of John Smith and the Puerto Rican salesman.

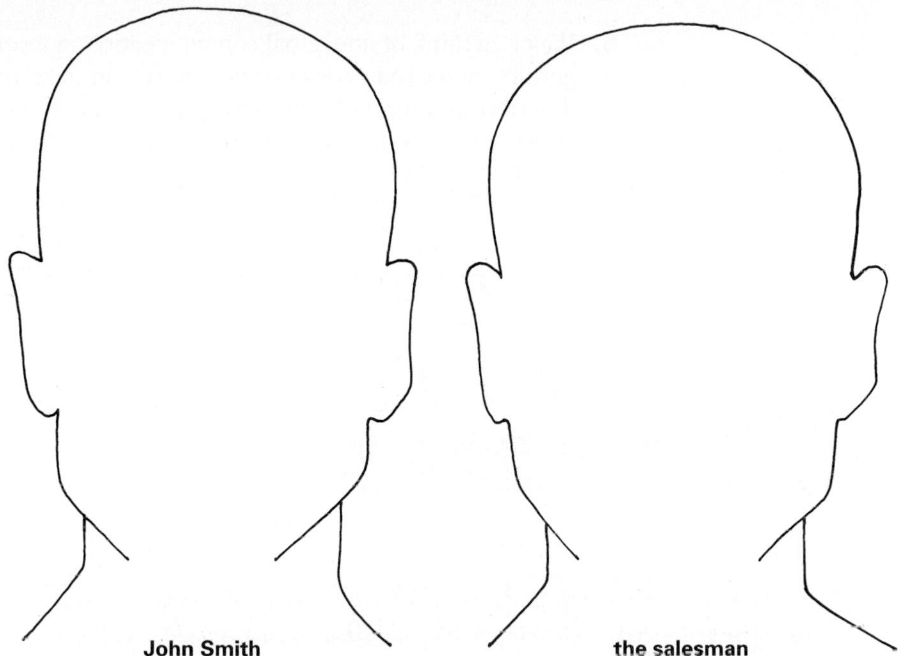

4. In his article, Fathi Yousef presents some useful technical terms for talking about nonverbal behavior. Look back at the selection and find the words and expressions in the following list. Try to guess their meanings by studying their contexts. Write your guesses, then check them by consulting your dictionary and your teacher.

a. a monochronic pattern of interpersonal communication

____

____

b. a polychronic concept of time ______________________

____

____

c. cultural expectations______________________________

____

____

d. monochronic segments

____

____

e. temporal cycles_________________________________

____

____

5. We often think of nonverbal communication in terms of body language—gestures and expressions that we can see. In the article, however, Yousef describes an aspect of nonverbal communication that is more abstract. Write in your own words the aspect of nonverbal communication that Yousef describes.

____

____

____

THINKING CRITICALLY

Distinguishing Fact from Opinion

It is important to distinguish between objective *fact* and subjective *opinion* or *interpretation*, especially when trying to communicate successfully with people from different cultures. A fact is an event that happened or something that is true. An opinion is what someone *thinks* or *believes* about a fact.

Indicate if the following sentences are *facts* by writing F or if they are *opinions* by writing O.

____ **Puerto Ricans are disorganized.**

____ **If you speak the language, you know how to communicate successfully.**

____ **Interrupting is always rude.**

____ **It is most efficient to serve more than one customer at a time.**

____ **It is not necessary for a salesman to greet each customer.**

If you wrote O for each sentence, you are right. Each of these is a subjective opinion. Now write three facts in the following space. Use the example to get started.

example: Successful communication includes knowledge of nonverbal as well as verbal language.

1.

2.

3.

Gathering Information

Complete one or more of the following activities.

1. Teach your classmates an example of nonverbal behavior commonly understood in your home country. You can teach a gesture or facial expression or demonstrate how people use and perceive time or space. Choose an aspect of nonverbal behavior that no one else has selected and spend some time planning your presentation.
2. Choose an example of nonverbal behavior and find out what it means in three different cultures. Interview your classmates, Americans, other foreigners in your community, or people from your own culture. Take notes and organize your information in the following chart.

nonverbal behavior	meaning: culture 1	meaning: culture 2	meaning: culture 3

3. Watch at least one half hour of an American television program or movie. Turn the sound down. Make a list of as many examples of nonverbal behavior as you can. Indicate what you think each one means. Record your information in the chart on the next page and share it with your classmates. *Note:* Soap operas, situation comedies, and dramatic/action programs are best for this exercise.

title of program or film	date and time	nonverbal behavior	possible meaning
Melrose Place	November 2, 9:00 PM	Man scratches head and raises eyebrows	He is confused.

PART two Language for Writing

Describing Nonverbal Behavior and Cultural Values

The following words and expressions are useful in describing nonverbal behavior. Each has to do with a particular body movement that has a meaning in North American culture. Study them in small groups. Take turns demonstrating them and explaining what they mean. If you are unsure, ask your teacher. Add your own new words and phrases on the lines at the bottom.

winking
bowing
hugging
shrugging your shoulders
standing close together

kissing
embracing
shaking hands
standing far apart

nodding your head
shaking your head
raising your eyebrows
making/having eye contact

Here are some words that express cultural values. Note that in this context, they are all uncountable. Can you think of any others? Add them on the lines below.

love
(dis)respect
gratitude

honor
politeness
(dis)agreement

Interpreting Nonverbal Behavior

The following expressions are useful for interpreting and observing behavior. Study the list. Then practice using the expressions by writing sentences of your own. Share your sentences with the class.

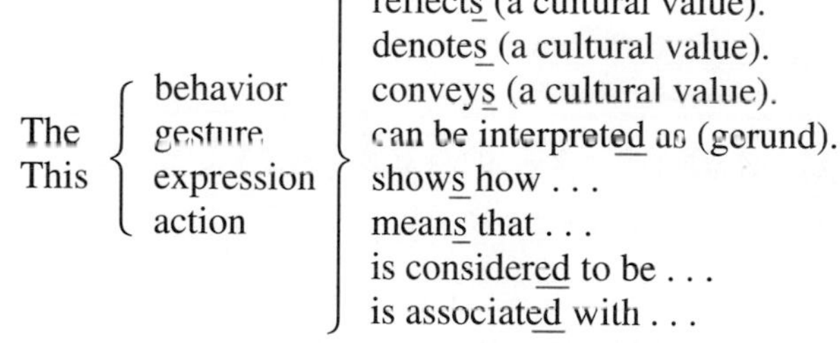

examples: This behavior reflects the importance of the family.
The action conveys respect for the elderly.
This action can be interpreted as showing affection.
The gesture is considered to be a sign of approval.

What other nouns could substitute for the word *behavior* in the preceding expressions (*action*, *gesture*, *facial expressions*, *movement*, *attitude*, and so forth)?

Practicing What You've Learned

Using the information you gathered in Part One, either draw five to ten pictures or diagrams of different examples of nonverbal behavior from another culture (not your own), or find pictures of them in magazines, newspapers, or photographs. Next to each picture, write a sentence describing the behavior. Use words and expressions you learned in this part, as well as some of your own.

example: An employee is sitting on another employee's desk in an office. This behavior shows how some Americans interact at work.

Write sentences like those in Exercise 1 describing nonverbal behavior in your own culture. Use words and expressions from this part.

example: In my culture, a student never makes eye contact with his or her teacher. To do so would convey disrespect. This denotes the great respect we hold for educators.

Choose three photos from the beginning of the chapter. Write at least two sentences describing each one. Use the behavior expressions to describe what the people are doing and the interpretation expressions to explain what cultural value the behavior reflects (what the behavior means).

example: Photo 3: Three Japanese women are bowing. This behavior denotes respect.

PART three
Systems for Writing

Review Point

Use listing signals and sentence connectors to make your paragraphs coherent.

Paragraph Development: General to Specific Information

New Points

- In a well-developed paragraph, the writer supports general statements with specific examples that are clear, relevant, and interesting.
- There are two basic ways to organize general-to-specific information in a paragraph.
  1. You can divide your topic into two or more parts and give specific information about the parts, thereby giving specific information about the main idea. In this book, we will call this a "divided" organizational pattern.
  2. You can take one main idea and go into great depth by giving more and more specific information about that one main idea. In this book, we will call this a "top-down" organizational pattern.
- The pattern you choose depends on what you are writing about.

A "divided" organizational pattern looks like this:

1 Topic sentence (most general: has two parts)
  2 First part (more specific)
    3 Fact or illustration related to the first part (very specific)
  2 Second part (same level of specificity as the first part)
    3 Fact or illustration related to the second part (very specific)

A "top-down" organizational pattern looks like this:

1 Topic sentence (most general idea)
  2 More specific information about the topic
    3 More specific information about sentence 2
      4 More specific information about sentence 3
        5 More specific information about sentence 4
          6 More specific information about sentence 5

Read the following paragraph on how city planners use space differently in different cultures. As you read, notice the way the writer has organized her ideas. When you finish, work with a partner and answer the questions on the next page.

(1) A major system for using space in city planning is called the "radiating star." (2) The star pattern is one in which lines radiate from a central point. (3) An example of this is in the city of Paris, at the Arc de Triomphe. (4) This monument has several streets and boulevards leading away from it on all sides, like the points of a star.

1. What is the topic of the first sentence? ______________________________

____

Is this sentence *general* or *specific?* ______________________________

2. What is the topic of sentence 4? ______________________________

____

Is it general or specific? ______________________________

3. Now look at sentences 2 and 3. Decide whether each one is more general or more specific than the sentence that comes before and write your answers below.

MORE GENERAL OR MORE SPECIFIC?

Sentence 2 ______________________________

Sentence 3 ______________________________

4. Which organizational pattern did you find in the paragraph?

____

Here's another paragraph that a student wrote on the subject of how space is used in different cultures. Read it and answer the questions that follow.

(1) There are two major systems for using space in city planning. (2) One is the "radiating star," where lines (avenues or roads) radiate from a central point. (3) The other is the "grid," in which the lines intersect each other, making a series of connecting squares. (4) There are many examples of the star system in France. (5) One is the Arc de Triomphe, a monument that has several streets and boulevards leading away from it on all sides like the points on a star. (6) The grid system is used throughout the United States. (7) New York City is a good example of this system. (8) Over a hundred numbered streets lie horizontally across the rectangular island of Manhattan, each of which is intersected vertically by a smaller number of boulevards.

1. What is the topic of the first sentence? ______________________________

____

How many *parts* does it have? ______________________________

Are these parts the *same* or *different* in terms of their level of generality?

____

2. What is the topic of sentence 2? ___

Is it more general or more specific than sentence 1? ___

___

3. What is the topic of sentence 6? ___

How does this sentence relate to sentence 1? ___

___

___

4. Now look at sentences 3, 4, 5, 7, and 8. Describe the relationship of each of these sentences to the other sentences around it. Consider whether it is more general or more specific.

Sentence 3: ___

Sentence 4: ___

Sentence 5: ___

Sentence 7: ___

Sentence 8: ___

5. Which organizational pattern did you find in this paragraph?

___

focus on testing

Using Organizational Patterns

When taking a test, it is sometimes helpful to use organizational patterns like the ones on page 181 to help you see the relationships between ideas. Writing down your organizational pattern will help keep your writing on topic. It will also remind you to include enough supporting information.

A student is going to write a paragraph about greetings. Following are her notes. First, she needs to organize them into categories. Then she needs to determine which ideas are general and which are specific. Try to help her by following the steps below and on the next page.

Step 1. What's the most general idea in the list? Write a "1" next to it.
Step 2. Find the two major divisions of the most general idea, and write "2" next to them.

Step 3. Finally, decide which category the specific examples fall into. Write "3a" next to the example that supports "a friend" and "3b" next to that which supports "a stranger."

_____ greeting a stranger

_____ greetings

_____ greeting a friend of the same sex

_____ greeting a friend

_____ greeting a stranger of the opposite sex

Here is another list of notes from a different student. Help this student organize them. Follow the same three steps you just did.

1. Write a "1" next to the most general idea.
2. Write "2" next to the two major divisions of the most general idea.
3. Write "3a" next to polite gestures or "3b" next to impolite gestures.

_____ gestures to get someone's attention in the United States

_____ polite gestures to get attention

_____ impolite gestures to get someone's attention

_____ waving one's hand

_____ making eye contact

_____ snapping one's fingers

A third student is going to write a paragraph about one aspect of nonverbal behavior in Japan. Read his notes below and arrange them in the order of *general to specific* by numbering the phrases from 1 (most general) to 6 (most specific).

_____ nonverbal communication in Japan

_____ the way I bow when I greet my professor

_____ greetings

_____ nonverbal communication

_____ bowing

_____ relative depth of bows

Outlines

New Points

Preparing an outline makes essay writing easier.

- An outline can be as simple as a list of your thesis statement and the topic sentences of each of the paragraphs you are planning to write.
- You can also make an outline more detailed, so that it includes all your supporting information (your ideas and examples) in short, note-like form.

Here is an example of one kind of outline that will help you with general-to-specific paragraph development. The supporting information is written in note form. Only some of the information is filled in. Read the student essay on the next page and fill in the missing information in the outline below. Use note form.

SHAU

Paragraph 1: Thesis statement: Shau = Chinese way of expressing love for parent through actions

Paragraph 2: 1 Analysis of the Chinese character
- 2 Two symbols
  - 3 First: offspring; second: a person being carried
    - 4
      - 5
        - 6
          - 7
            - 8

Paragraph 3: 1 Story about Shen
- 2 Shen was considerate of parents
  - 3
    - 3
- 2 Shen expressed love through actions

Paragraph 4: 1 Examples of shau
- 2
  - 3
- 2
  - 3
- 2
  - 3

Paragraph 5: Conclusion: Restatement of thesis

Shau

Do you know that the Chinese who are not influenced by western culture rarely, if ever, say "I love you" to their parents? In fact, they never say anything to their parents that is equivalent to the words "I love you." Why do you suppose the Chinese don't say "I love you" to their parents? It's certainly not because they don't love their parents but because a more acceptable way of expressing love for parents is by action. Because this love is unlike other kinds of love for other people, naturally there is a special word for it. This word in Chinese is *shau,* which means "love for parents expressed in action."

(1) Perhaps the word *shau* is better understood by analyzing the character we use to write it. (2) The character *shau* is made up of two symbols. (3) The first, which symbolizes a son or, more precisely, offspring, is underneath the second symbol, which represents a person being carried. (4) Together, the two symbols represent a son carrying his father. (5) Whoever invented this word was probably inspired by the scene of a good son carrying his weak old father who can't walk well. (6) This act by the son shows how much he loves his father. (7) He willingly sacrifices his youthful energy and time to serve his father. (8) *Shau* encompasses all forms of active love for parents.

(1) *Shau* is illustrated in a classic Chinese story about a young man named Shen. (2) Shen was very considerate of his parents. (3) In summer, before his parents took a nap, he would cool his parents' bed by fanning it, so that they could sleep comfortably. (3) During the winter, before his parents went to bed, he would lie in their bed long enough to make the bed and cover warm, so that his parents would not suffer from winter cold. (2) Shen didn't need to tell his parents that he loved them because his love for them was obvious through his actions.

(1) *Shau,* which is a loving act to parents by a son or a daughter, is best understood by example. (2) For instance, *shau* is not forgetting about your parents' health. (2) *Shau* is waking up at two o'clock in the morning to remind your mother to take her medicine. (2) *Shau* is not visiting parents on the weekend when you don't have better things to do. (3) *Shau* is taking time off work to spend time with your parents. (2) *Shau* is not sending your parents away to an old people's apartment, so that they won't ask you to run errands. (3) *Shau* is letting your parents live in your house, so that you can be at their service when they need you.

Therefore, *shau* is love for parents expressed by action. This action is out of a willingness to sacrifice oneself on behalf of one's parents. To some extent, *shau* is an endeavor to love our parents in the same way that they have loved us ever since we were born. They sacrifice time and money to love us the best way they know how. *Shau* is just a return of this kind of love.

Practicing What You've Learned

exercise 1

Choose a set of notes from the three exercises on pages 183 and 184 and write a paragraph by expanding the notes into sentences. Use the order that you established by numbering each sentence. In addition, number the sentences using the same numbers you used in the notes: 1, 2, 3a, 3b. When you've finished, exchange paragraphs with a partner and double-check your ordering.

Write a short paragraph by expanding the notes from the last exercise on page 184 into sentences. Use the general-to-specific order and number your sentences. When you finish, exchange paragraphs with a partner and double-check your ordering.

Now that you have practiced how to develop paragraphs by supporting general statements with specific information, take a look at the following groups of sentences. Try to figure out what is missing. Then use the sentences to write paragraphs by supplying the missing elements. Number your sentences when you've finished.

1. Both travel and study in a foreign country have important advantages. One is intellectual growth. The other is emotional growth.
2. Many people pursue hobbies in their leisure time. One popular hobby is collecting things. Some people collect useful art objects.

Read the following example of a well-developed paragraph on the two main purposes of eye contact in the United States. First, draw an outline of its general-to-specific structure. Then, using the same structure, write an outline and a paragraph of your own about two functions of eye contact in your culture or any other you are familiar with. Your paragraph may have *more* than eight sentences, but make sure that it doesn't have fewer.

> There are two main purposes of eye contact in the United States: getting someone's attention and indicating that you are listening to a speaker. Using eye contact is a way of getting someone's attention in a public place. The most common use of this is getting the attention of a waiter or waitress in a busy restaurant. The technique is to locate your waiter, watch him carefully, and as soon as he turns in your direction, look at him directly in the eyes.

He'll soon come over to take your order or give you your bill. Using eye contact is equally important in North America to show a speaker that you are paying attention. The general American rule for conversational eye contact is to look at the speaker's eyes the entire time he or she is speaking—that is, having his or her turn in the conversation. This tells the speaker "I'm listening to you"; to look away even for a few seconds may make the speaker think that you are bored.

Writing Assignments

Write an essay on one of the following topics. Use new vocabulary and expressions you learned in this chapter and make sure that your paragraphs are clear and coherent. Develop your ideas by using information from the research you did in Part One.

1. Describe and interpret three examples of nonverbal behavior in a particular culture. Be sure to explain the behavior in terms of the cultural values it represents. You can discuss nonverbal behavior in your culture or any other you are familiar with.
2. Illustrate the nonverbal aspects of a particular kind of social interaction in three different cultures. You may wish to choose one of the following:
   a. Greeting a friend of the same sex
   b. Greeting a friend of the opposite sex
   c. Showing respect
   d. Greeting a stranger
   e. Insulting someone
3. Show how nonverbal behavior can cause cross-cultural misunderstanding.
4. Show the differences or similarities in nonverbal behavior in two cultures. You can compare your own culture with U.S./Canadian culture, or you can choose any two cultures that interest you.
5. Agree with, disagree with, or explain the following quotation:

   "Probably no more than thirty to thirty-five percent of the social meaning of a conversation or interaction is carried by the words."
   —*Ray Birdwhistell*, American anthropologist

6. Write an essay about any aspect of nonverbal behavior that interests you.

Evaluating for Rewriting

Working with Your Partner

step 1

Exchange the essays you wrote for the Writing Assignments section. Use the following questionnaire to evaluate each other's essays.

1. Read the first sentence of each paragraph of the body of the essay without reading the rest of it. What organizational pattern do you think each one is going to follow?

   a. Top-down 1 2 3 4 etc. — or — b. Divided 1 2 3 2 3

   Paragraph 1 _____ Paragraph 2 _____ Paragraph 3 _____

   What is the main idea expressed in the first sentence of each body paragraph?

   Paragraph 1: ______________________________

   Paragraph 2: ______________________________

   Paragraph 3: ______________________________

2. Now read the rest of each paragraph. Were your answers to question 1 correct?

   Paragraph 1 yes _____ no _____

   Paragraph 2 yes _____ no _____

   Paragraph 3 yes _____ no _____

3. Number the sentences in the paragraphs of the body to show how each relates to the preceding one. Was this easy or difficult to do? Why?

   Paragraph 1: ______________________________

   ____

   Paragraph 2: ______________________________

   ____

   Paragraph 3: ______________________________

   ____

4. How many level-3 sentences (facts and illustrations) did body paragraph 1 have? _____

Briefly list the level-3 sentences used in this paragraph:

Were there any level-2 sentences not followed by level-3 sentences? If so, make suggestions for improvement:

How many level-3 sentences did body paragraph 2 have? _____

Briefly list the level-3 sentences used in this paragraph:

Were there any level-2 sentences not followed by level-3 sentences? If so, make suggestions for improvement:

How many level-3 sentences did body paragraph 3 have? _____

Briefly list the level-3 sentences used in this paragraph:

Were there any level-2 sentences not followed by level-3 sentences? If so, make suggestions for improvement:

5. Were there any level-4 sentences or level-5 sentences in these paragraphs? What were they?

Paragraph 1:

Paragraph 2:

Paragraph 3:

Return each other's essays. Read your partner's evaluation of your essay. Discuss any questions you have with your partner.

Working on Your Own

Now you should be ready to evaluate your own paper. Go through the questions again. Take into consideration what your partner said about your paper when he or she evaluated it. Is there more to add? Words to change?

Rewrite your essay, making any necessary changes. Turn this revised draft of your essay in to your teacher.

CHAPTER ten

Crime and Punishment

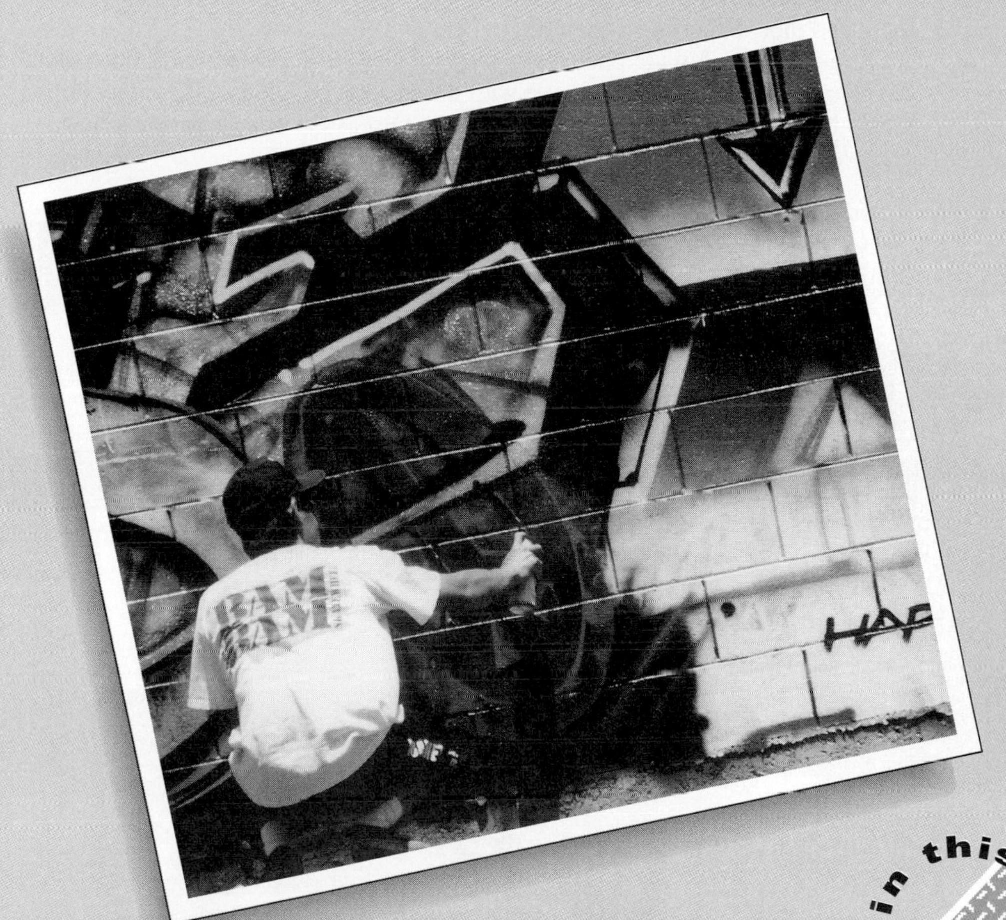

in this chapter

You will debate an issue related to crime and punishment and write a summary and reaction to a controversial issue.

PART one
Ideas for Writing

Getting Started

Many Americans are concerned about increased crime and violence. They feel unsafe in their own homes and neighborhoods. What are some ways to reduce crime? What controversial issues surround the subject of crime and punishment?

In this chapter, you will examine some of these controversial issues. You will practice stating an opinion on a controversial issue related to crime and punishment and then defending it in writing.

Look at the following photos and read each of the accompanying statements in the chart. Do you agree or disagree with them? Indicate your opinion by circling the appropriate number on the opinion scale. Discuss your opinions in small groups and give reasons for your answers.

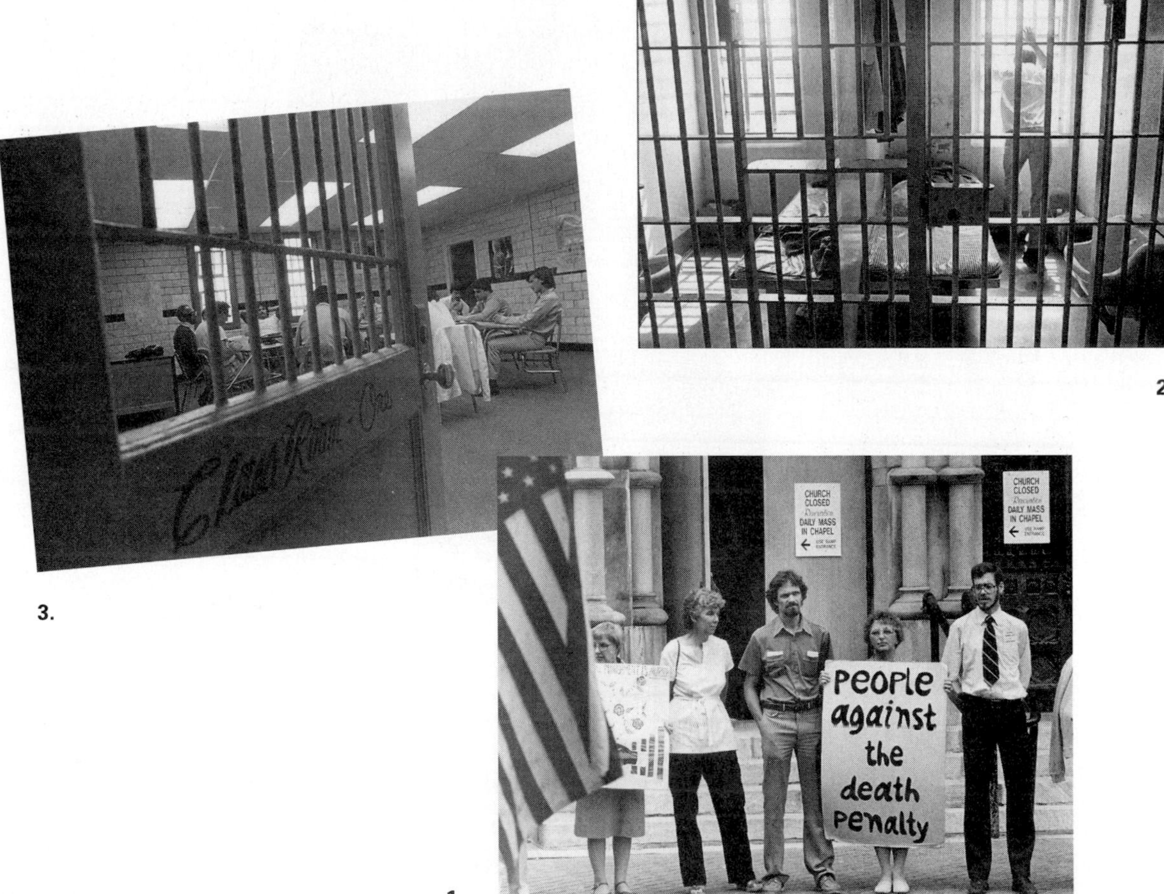

2.

3.

1.

4.

5.

6.

statements	opinion scale strongly agree → strongly disagree			
1. The death penalty discourages crime.	1	2	3	4
2. Prisons reduce crime.	1	2	3	4
3. Prisoners can be rehabilitated.	1	2	3	4
4. Juveniles should be tried and punished the same way as adults are.	1	2	3	4
5. There would be less crime if more parents spanked their children.	1	2	3	4
6. Community service is a good alternative to prison.	1	2	3	4

Brainstorming

Study the photos on pages 194 and 195 and think about the themes they represent. The statements that accompany them in the chart (page 195) suggest controversial issues, but there are many more controversies surrounding crime and punishment that may interest you. Think of additional arguable statements for the following issues and write them in the chart. The first one is done as an example.

issue	controversial statement
1. The death penalty	The death penalty doesn't discourage crime.
2. Prisons for punishment	
3. Prisons for rehabilitation	
4. Juvenile crime	
5. Alternatives to prison	
6. Your issue: ____________	

Freewriting

It is often easier to talk and write about something you feel strongly about than an issue on which you are neutral. Choose an issue regarding crime and punishment you feel strongly about, and discuss your opinion by writing for fifteen minutes without stopping.

Reading for Ideas

In 1994, a 17-year old American was convicted of vandalism in Singapore. His punishment was to receive four strikes on bare skin with a cane (a wooden stick). Public opinion polls showed that many Americans felt caning was too harsh a punishment for the crime; however, many others supported the punishment, a kind that does not exist in the United States. William J. Bennett, a former member of President Bush's cabinet, wrote an essay for *Newsweek* magazine to explain why some Americans supported such an extreme form of punishment and to offer some suggestions for improving the justice system in America.

Before you read the essay, answer the following questions in small groups.

prereading questions

1. Share any knowledge you have on how youth are punished for crimes around the world. Which countries allow corporal punishment (flogging, caning, beating)?
2. Discuss different methods of disciplining children. Consider cultural differences in your group (if any) in how children are disciplined or trained in correct behavior.
3. Share your definition of "justice."
4. Discuss this question: Do you feel safe on the streets in the country you are currently living in? Why or why not?
5. The vocabulary in this reading is more difficult than that of previous selections. Look up and discuss the following words before you read; other words (in italics) appear in a glossary at the end of the passage.

endorse	anarchy
embrace	sidestepped
vandalism	authoritarian
prudence	backlash
floggings	tranquility
fidelity	regeneration
red tape	

Raising Cain on Values
Discipline: Spare the Rod—But Crack Down

By William J. Bennett

In light of America's terrible crime and its *floundering* legal system, the impulse to side with the Singaporean government and endorse caning is understandable. But it is also wrong. Our weakness should not lead us to embrace unnecessary cruelty.

At the same time . . . the public's pro-caning *sentiment* is tied to a growing, *justifiable* outrage . . . at what is happening to modern American society. People are frustrated because government is failing to carry out its first responsibility: to provide for the security of its citizens. . . .

Over the last three decades violent crime has increased by more than 500 percent. America leads the industrialized world in rates of murder, rape and violent crime. Nearly three out of every four convicted criminals are not *incarcerated*. Fewer than one in 10 serious crimes results in imprisonment. . . .

It isn't surprising, then, that many Americans look at what Singapore has achieved with admiration. But Singapore is not the type of authoritarian society to which we should *aspire*. I am all in favor of *dispensing* tough punishment; I was a very strong *advocate* of "law and order" policies when I was President Bush's "drug czar," and I still am. But there is a responsible middle ground between *tepidness* and torture. It is on that ground that American society should stand. After all, it is ground we once occupied, and which we can occupy again.

Here's the essential point: to see justice administered, we don't have to see people strapped, their skin raked, and flesh fly. Public floggings aren't necessary to establish safe streets. Our choice is not between red tape and red blood.

If not caning-like punishment, what ought we to do? First, we desperately need to reform our criminal justice system. Punishment needs to be swifter, more certain and longer than it is now. We need to do the *prosaic*: build more prisons, hire more police and prosecutors, . . .and overhaul our juvenile justice system, among other things. In the case of. . .vandalism, punishment by prison term and fine should do it. If U.S. vandalism was regularly punished by imprisonment and fine, is there any doubt that it would diminish?

The larger challenge is how to keep young people from ever falling into the criminal-justice system in the first place. We now ask prisons to do what fathers once did and ask the entire criminal-justice system to do what parents, schools and neighborhoods once did.

A hard *indictment* of our time is: during the last quarter century, many parents, schools, churches and communities sidestepped their obligations and passed off parental, familial and communal responsibility to government. But government, no matter how sincere, cannot do this job.

The task of parents and other adults with responsibility for the young consists of moral training and supervision. That, in turn, consists of teaching by rules and precepts, but most of all, it means teaching by example. It means providing order and loving discipline. At home, might this involve an expertly wielded rattan cane? No. Spanking? Occasionally. Parents know a spank or a slap is often a quick reflex that might bring temporary *respite*. But it is no substitute for the better elements of parental and moral guidance: logging lots of time doing chores and errands, playing together, reading together, doing homework together, and patiently explaining the way the world works and the way people—mothers, fathers and children—ought to live and how they fall short.

More broadly, as a society we simply need to become more civilized. I say "simply" because there is a tendency to over-intellectualize our task or to throw up our hands in despair. Intelligent, tough-minded public policies can help achieve greater domestic tranquility. But in the end, regeneration in a free society must come from within. We need to *revivify* old republican virtues like self-control, prudence, honor and fidelity to commitments.

The American public will not accept indefinitely widespread lawlessness. If violent crime continues to rise, if the human *carnage* continues to mount, then we will look for someone on horseback with a rattan cane or something much worse to restore order. Our free democratic institutions cannot withstand much more crime without a terrible counterreaction. Social anarchy often triggers an authoritarian backlash. When people are sick and tired, the whip has its appeal. Let's give our citizens another option, rooted in the ideal of justice and the traditions of a civilized society: punishment that recognizes the requirements of lawful order, safe communities and human dignity—and a system that teaches clear and firm lessons and is itself a good example to our children.

William J. Bennett

GLOSSARY

floundering—struggling or losing control
sentiment—feeling
justifiable—understandable
incarcerated—jailed
aspire—want to become
dispensing—giving
advocate—supporter
tepidness—weakness
prosaic—dull; uninteresting
indictment—a formal charge of wrongdoing
respite—rest
revivify—bring back
carnage—killing

postreading questions

1. According to Bennett, why did many Americans support the Singaporean government when it caned a young American who committed vandalism?

___

___

___

2. What is Bennett's opinion of Singaporean society in general, and its use of caning as a form of punishment in particular? Do you agree with him? Why or why not? ___

___

___

___

3. What suggestions does Bennett make for reforming the criminal justice system in the United States? Do you agree with his suggestions? Why or why not? ___

___

___

___

4. What punishment does Bennett propose for vandalism in the United States? Do you agree with his suggestion? Why or why not? ___

___

___

___

5. What suggestions does Bennett make to parents for improving the moral training of children? Do you think these practices would reduce juvenile crime? Why or why not? ___

___

___

___

6. In paragraph 10, what values does Bennett imply that Americans have lost? Do you agree with him? How important are these values to you personally? In your culture? What values has your native culture lost, if any?

____

____

____

7. In paragraph 11, Bennett states that social anarchy "often triggers an authoritarian backlash." Do you agree? Why or why not? Give examples to support your opinion. ______________________

____

____

____

THINKING CRITICALLY

Recognizing Provable Statements

Magazine and newspaper writers often make controversial statements about social issues. In order to think clearly about these statements, it's a good idea to know which are provable—that is, ones that can be supported by factual evidence—and which are unprovable—those that cannot be proved (because they are opinions or rumors, for example). Obviously, you can take the provable statements more seriously.

Look at these examples from Bennett's essay. The second statement is provable; you can do research to verify the statistics the author uses. The first statement isn't—it's the author's personal opinion.

1. **We need to revivify old republican virtues like self-control, prudence, honor and fidelity to commitments.**
2. **Over the last three decades violent crime has increased by more than 500 percent.**

Work with a partner and find two more provable statements and two more unprovable ones in Bennett's essay. You and your partner may not agree; be prepared to discuss the reasons for your choices.

Gathering Information

You are going to hold a debate with your classmates—a formal discussion of a controversial issue. This debate will help you prepare for your writing assignment later in the chapter.

In a debate, two teams or two speakers each represent opposing sides of an issue. They try to convince the audience that their position is the better one by clearly presenting arguments supporting their position and anticipating counter-arguments from the other side.

Most debates have the following structure:

DEBATE

- **I.** Resolution
- **II.** Opening statement
- **III.** First argument and supports; rebuttal
- **IV.** Second argument and supports; rebuttal
- **V.** Third argument and supports; rebuttal
- **VI.** Closing statement

Complete the following steps to prepare for your debate.

Step 1. As a class, decide on an issue to debate. Select one of the issues related to crime and punishment that you discussed at the beginning of the chapter. It must be debatable—that is, the issue must have two opposing sides that you can support. Turn your topic into a resolution and write it on the board. Here is a sample resolution:

Topic: The death penalty.
Resolution: The death penalty discourages crime.

As you can see, this resolution presents the "pro" side of the argument. What is the "con" side?

Step 2. Now that you have a resolution, divide into pro and con teams. Join the team that represents your true feelings about the issue, or choose the opposite side—just for the mental exercise!

Step 3. Choose one of the following debate team roles. If there aren't enough roles for all team members, additional people can help with the note taking, and two people can take the argument and rebuttal roles.

- **a.** *Team captain:* Leads the group and presents the opening and closing statements.
- **b.** *Secretary:* Takes notes on what everyone says during the planning stage and during the debate itself.
- **c.** *Three people who present arguments:* Each presents one of the main arguments for that side.
- **d.** *Three people who make opposing arguments:* Each presents a counterargument to the three main arguments given by the other side.

Step 4. Gather information to support your side of the topic. Consult resources in the library. Refer to articles, magazines, or books, as you would for an essay. Work with your team to develop your opening statement, your main arguments, your rebuttals and your closing. Before you start gathering information, look at the purpose of each segment of the debate, (outlined in step 5) so you'll know how much and what kind of information you'll need.

Step 5. The debate will take about forty-five to sixty minutes. You and your teacher can decide on the actual time for each segment. Use the following format as a guideline:

Team: Pro and Con

	purpose	time
Opening argument	Clearly states team's position on the issue.	1 minute
Three arguments	Represent the three main supports for team's position. You must develop each argument with facts, statistics, and examples, just as you do in an essay. Facts and statistics are the most important support devices.	3 minutes each
Three rebuttals	Counterarguments to the other team's three main arguments. Try to predict what the other side's three main arguments will be. Then think of the opposing points of view and develop each one as you did for your main arguments. Break time during the debate will allow you to change your rebuttals if your predictions weren't right.	3 minutes each
Closing statement	Restates your position.	1 minute

Note the suggested times for each part. Take three-to-five-minute breaks after each side's arguments so that the people presenting rebuttals can make changes if necessary.

Step 6. Decide who won the debate by having the presenters and or the audience vote for the side that was more convincing. Also, take the time for a follow-up discussion on how you felt about the debate.

Language for Writing

Citing Authorities

As you saw in Chapter Five, it's a good idea to cite or quote authorities in your essays, and it is essential to refer to other writers when you are responding to another piece of writing. In English there are certain conventions for citing sources. First, use the full name of the person you quote or refer to the first time you mention him or her. Use the last name only after that.

example: In "Raising Cain on Values," William Bennett asserts that America needs to change its criminal justice system. For example, Bennett suggests that we extend sentences, build more prisons, and hire more police, among other things.

(Remember to put titles of articles in quotation marks and underline or italicize titles of books and films.)

The following list contains the most common words and expressions used to cite, or refer to, another author. Each conveys a slightly different meaning. Discuss them with your teacher.

X (the original author) { states / claims / alleges / says / explains / writes / asserts / indicates / maintains } that . . .

According to X, . . .

example: According to William Bennett, Americans are frustrated by the government's inability to provide security to its citizens.

Note the difference between citing authorities and using direct quotes. See Part Two, Chapter Five for reviewing material on using quotations.

Exposing Weaknesses in Opposing Arguments

In writing an argument essay, you need to make convincing arguments that support your side of the issue. However, you also need to recognize arguments on the *other* side of the issue—that is, arguments that are *opposed* to your position. An effective strategy for making your arguments stronger is to expose weaknesses in these opposing arguments—for example, by predicting how the other side's arguments may have negative results. One way to do this is by using conditional sentences. The following are three examples.

- If prisoners are not rehabilitated, they will never lead productive lives in the outside world.
- Young offenders will become hardened criminals if they are treated as adults by the criminal justice system.
- If a state abolishes the death penalty, it is sending the message that you can kill and get away with it.

Note that each of these sentences can be divided into two parts. One part is called the *condition clause* (introduced by *if*), and the other part is called the *result* clause.

Answer the following questions about the three example sentences you just read.

1. Note the position of the *if* condition clause. Does it come at the beginning of the sentence or at the end? ______________________________

____

2. Note the punctuation of the sentences. What is the rule about the position of the *if* condition clause and the use of commas?

____

____

3. Reread the *if* condition clauses in the sentences again. In terms of the *information* they contain, what do they all have in common?

____

____

4. Note the verb tense used in the *if* condition clauses. Is it always the same? What tense is it? ______________________________

____

Another way to write the example sentences is to use relative clauses, as follows:

- Prisoners who are not rehabilitated will never lead productive lives in the outside world.
- Young offenders who are treated as adults by the criminal justice system will become hardened criminals.
- A state that abolishes the death penalty is sending the message that you can kill and get away with it.

Note that these sentences using relative clauses mean the same as the conditional sentences in the previous examples. Using these kinds of sentences to expose weaknesses in opposing arguments gives strength to your own arguments and makes your writing more convincing.

Practicing What You've Learned

Answer the following questions by paraphrasing the ideas from previous reading selections. Cite the sources. Vary your responses and use what you've learned from this section.

1. How does David feel about being in Japan? (Chapter One)
2. What kind of health problems do many angry, cynical people have? (Chapter Four)
3. What attracts immigrants to Silicon Valley? (Chapter Six)
4. What do you think should be the main goal of the Olympic Games? (Chapter Seven)
5. How does one learn to be creative? (Chapter Eight)
6. What can lead to a breakdown in cross-cultural communication? (Chapter Nine)

Write a paragraph based on research you did for the debate in Part One. Cite sources correctly.

Choose three quotations from Writing Assignments sections of any of the previous chapters: For each quotation, write two sentences. In the first sentence, repeat the quotation and cite the source. In the second sentence, paraphrase the quotation.

Use your own opinions to complete the following sentences by providing the missing clause or by rewriting the sentence with a relative clause. Don't forget to add punctuation where necessary.

example: if prisons rehabilitate rather than punish
If prisons rehabilitate rather than punish, prisoners will become productive, law-abiding citizens.
or
Prisoners who are rehabilitated rather than punished in prison will become productive, law-abiding citizens.

1. if ______________________ (country, state) abolishes the death penalty

____

____

____

2. young people will be less likely to commit crimes ____________________

____

____

____

3. violent crime will continue to increase ____________________________

____

____

____

4. if the criminal justice system in ______________ (country) isn't reformed

____

____

____

5. vandalism will continue to increase ____________________________

____

____

____

exercise 5

Write five sentences of your own, but take the *opposite* point of view from the previous exercise. Try to vary the sentences as much as possible. Exchange sentences with a partner and check each other's work when you finish.

example: Prisoners who are punished rather than rehabilitated in prison will become productive, law-abiding citizens.

1. ____

____

2. ____

____

3. ____

____

4. ____

____

5. ____

____

Write a paragraph about the issue you selected in the Freewriting section of Part One, page 196. Include the opposing point of view in condition clauses.

PART three
Systems for Writing

Review Point

When you paraphrase something, you restate it in your own words.

Summarizing

New Points

- The purpose of a summary is to explain in an economical way something that someone else has written.
- A summary is shorter than the original work but contains all the main ideas of the original.
- Since you often have to restate information from the source you are summarizing, paraphrasing is an important part of summarizing.

Read this summary of the essay by William J. Bennett from Part One. Then answer the questions that follow.

According to William J. Bennett, if America doesn't renew its commitment to lost values, it is in danger of losing its status as a civilized society. In "Raising Cain on Values," Bennett claims that Americans are justifiably fed up with the rise in lawlessness in the United States. He relates some recent crime statistics as evidence of the growing threat of violent crime in the United States. Bennett does not agree with some Americans, however, that instituting the extreme forms of punishment that some countries employ is the answer to this problem. Rather, he suggests a middle road and proposes reforms in the United States' current justice system, such as swifter sentencing and longer prison terms. He also suggests that greater parental involvement in the lives of children will reduce youth crime. Bennett concludes by lamenting the fact that Americans have lost the values that once made their society strong, and he states that strengthening the criminal justice system will again make the United States the civilized society it once was.

1. How long is the original article? How long is the summary?

____

2. What is the purpose of the first sentence of the summary? What information does it contain?

____

____

____

____

3. Look at the original article in Part One. How many main ideas are there? What are they? Now look at the summary. Are the same main ideas discussed? Are any missing?

____

____

____

____

____

4. Note the order of the ideas in the original. Is the same order used in the summary? ________________________________

____

____

5. Note the use of details, facts, and illustrations in the original article. Do many of these details appear in the summary? Why or why not?

____

____

6. Whose ideas are expressed in the summary? How do you know? Do any opinions appear in the summary that are not in the original article? Why or why not? ______________________________

____

____

____

____

____

7. Find examples of the language the writer of the summary uses to refer to Bennett's ideas and underline them.

8. Does the writer of the summary copy or paraphrase words and expressions Bennett uses? Find examples of both cases.

____

____

____

Based on your answers to the preceding questions, what are some guidelines for writing a good summary? Write them below.

____

____

____

____

____

____

____

____

____

____

Organizing a Summary-and-Reaction Essay

New Points

- In a summary-and-reaction essay, you respond to something that someone else has written or said.
- In this kind of essay, you summarize the main points of the speech or article in the first paragraph, concluding with your reaction, which serves as your thesis statement.
- The rest of the essay develops your thesis statement.

A summary-and-reaction essay looks like this:

Paragraph 1:	Summary of essay you are reacting to Last sentence: your thesis (that is, your opinion on what the author has to say)
Paragraph 2:	Body: Support for your thesis
Paragraph 3:	Body: Support for your thesis
Paragraph 4:	Body (optional): Support for your thesis
Paragraph 5:	Conclusion

Note that, instead of an introduction, you lead up to your thesis with a summary of the article you are going to react to. Your thesis presents *your* point of view—either agreement or disagreement with the author or both—and the body paragraphs explain your reasons for thinking the way you do.

focus on testing

Writing a Quick Summary and Reaction

You are often asked to react to a reading on standardized tests. Using the organizational pattern above will help you quickly compose a good response to a summary-and-reaction essay question.

Practicing What You've Learned

Read the following article, "Time to Ban Styrofoam?" Then read the three summaries. Only one of the summaries is accurate and well written. First, find the good summary. Then, explain what's wrong with the remaining two by referring to the questions about the Bennett summary on pages 208 and 209.

Time to Ban Styrofoam?

How much is convenience worth to you? Is the opportunity to keep your coffee hot in a styrofoam cup worth eventual skin cancer for you or your kids? Would you trade it for the melting of the polar ice caps?

On September 22, 1987, in Berkeley, California, the city council gave preliminary approval to an ordinance to ban styrofoam products manufactured with chloro-fluorocarbons, or CFCs. The nationwide attention to this simple move suggests that the idea may be one whose time has come. With the landfills filling up, and the ozone layer disintegrating year by year, it may be time for all of us to kick the styrofoam habit.

Hole in the Ozone

Chloro-fluorocarbons were first introduced in the 1930s as refrigerants and still continue to be used widely in refrigerators and air conditioners. They are an ideal "fluffing agent" in the manufacture of polystyrene foam: they puff up the plastic, which gives it its famous insulting properties. Another agent, pentane, is available, but it is highly flammable and oxidizes quickly in sunlight.

During the manufacturing process, about 90 percent of the CFCs are emitted into the air. The rest escape during storage, use, and destruction (if that occurs). Once airborne, they rise to the stratosphere, where they live for up to one hundred years destroying the ozone, the thin layer that protects the earth from the sun's damaging ultraviolet radiation.

What's ozone to you or me? Intact, the ozone layer screens out 99 percent of the sun's ultraviolet rays. For every 1 percent reduction in the ozone layer, another 2 percent of ultraviolet rays reach the ground, and for every 1 percent increase in ultraviolet rays, there are as many as 30,000 extra cases of skin cancer in the United States.

Berkeley's Historic Ban

The city of Berkeley has moved to ban the styrofoam containers used in fast-food restaurants that unnecessarily contribute CFCs to the atmosphere. The unanimously adopted ban calls for the voluntary cooperation of take-out food vendors to eliminate CFC-processed packaging in five months. The city council has also instructed city departments to no longer buy CFC-processed products. Styrofoam is a short-term convenience product, with health and environmental effects that are very long term.

Paul Rauber

A. On September 22 in Berkeley, California, the city council banned the use of styrofoam products. During the manufacturing of products, a large amount of CFCs are emitted into the air. This will result in the reduction in atmospheric ozone, which will in turn cause skin cancer. The time has come to ban the manufacture of styrofoam products and to stop sacrificing health for short-term convenience.

____

____

____

____

B. The article "Time To Ban Styrofoam?" discusses the issue of the legal use of chloro-fluorocarbons, or CFCs. In September, Berkeley, California, became the first city to respond to this universal problem by banning all styrofoam products. The convenience of using styrofoam was overruled because of its deadly effect on our environment. Once the CFCs are airborne, they rise to the stratosphere, where they destroy the ozone, the thin layer that protects the earth from the sun's damaging ultraviolet radiation. When 1 percent of the ozone layer is reduced, 2 percent more ultraviolet rays reach the ground. The dramatic increase in ultraviolet rays has caused 30,000 additional cases of skin cancer in the United States alone. In Berkeley, the ban of all CFC-processed products will become law soon. For our own benefit and that of our children, cooperation is needed to administer the ordinance.

____

____

____

C. In his article "Time to Ban Styrofoam?" Paul Rauber urges us to sacrifice the convenience of styrofoam containers because they pose a serious threat to the environment. He praises the recent ordinance by the Berkeley City Council aimed at banning styrofoam products manufactured with CFCs. These chloro-fluorocarbons are widely used as refrigerants and insulation in plastic. Their continued use, however, is dangerous for us and our environment. Rauber claims that during manufacturing, storage, and later disposal, CFCs are emitted into the air where they rise to the stratosphere and destroy the ozone layer. This layer protects the earth from ultraviolet radiation and prevents us from getting skin cancer. Rauber asserts that the time has come to ban the use of styrofoam products and to stop sacrificing health for short-term convenience.

____

____

____

Write summaries of the following articles. As you write, keep in mind the guidelines for summary writing and use the expressions for citing the original author whenever it is appropriate. Each summary should be about one paragraph in length.

1. Summarize the article "Cynicism and Mistrust Tied to Early Death," pages 76 and 77, Chapter Four.
2. Summarize the article on micromachines, pages 94 and 95, Chapter Five.
3. Write a summary of the newspaper article "Valley Visionaries," pages 114 and 115, Chapter Six.
4. Write a summary of "Nonverbal Behavior: Some Intricate and Diverse Dimensions in Intercultural Communication," by Fathi Yousef, pages 173 and 174, Chapter Nine.
5. Summarize an article of your choice. The article can be from a textbook, newspaper, or magazine. Make sure you can summarize the main idea of the article in one paragraph.

Writing Assignments

Write a four- or five-paragraph essay on one of the following topics. Use new vocabulary and expressions you learned from this chapter and make sure that your paragraphs are clear and coherent. Develop your ideas by using information from the research you did in Part One.

1. Argue for or against the issue you debated in class or another issue in Part One.
2. Agree with, disagree with, or explain one of the following quotations:

   "If you reject the food, ignore the customs, fear the religion, and avoid the people, you might better stay home. You are like a pebble thrown into water; you become wet on the surface but you are never a part of the water." *—James Michener*

   "History teaches us that it is not the rebels or the dissidents who endanger society but rather the unthinking, the unquestioning, the obedient, the silent, and the indifferent." *—Leon Litwack*

3. Write a summary of and react to one of the articles you read when you did your research for Part One.

4. Summarize and respond to an article from a newspaper or magazine on any controversial issue.

PART four
Evaluating for Rewriting

Working with Your Partner

step 1

Exchange the essays you wrote for the Writing Assignments section. Use the following questionnaire to evaluate each other's essays.

1. Find the thesis. Write it here.

   ____

   ____

2. If the introduction is a summary, is it easy to follow and does the thesis respond to it? If not, suggest how the writer can improve it.

   Yes No ______________________________________

   ____

3. Look at the topic sentences of the body paragraphs. Do they directly support the thesis? If not, how could they be improved?

   Topic Sentence 1 yes no ______________________

   Topic Sentence 2 yes no ______________________

   Topic Sentence 3 yes no ______________________

4. Read the body paragraphs. Rate the following features by circling + or –. Give the writer specific suggestions when possible.

	UNITY	ORGANIZATION	COHERENCE	SPECIFIC DETAILS
Paragraph 1:	+ –	+ –	+ –	+ –
Paragraph 2:	+ –	+ –	+ –	+ –
Paragraph 3:	+ –	+ –	+ –	+ –

5. Are there any unanswered questions at the end of the essay? If yes, how can the writer explain his or her point(s) more thoroughly?

   Yes No ______________________________________

   ____

6. Rate the entire essay, keeping in mind all the material you've learned in this chapter as well as in previous chapters.

Return each other's essays. Read your partner's evaluation of your essay. Discuss any questions you have with your partner.

Working on Your Own

step 1

Now you should be ready to evaluate your own essay. Go through the questions again. Take into consideration what your partner said about your thesis statement when he or she evaluated it. Does it adequately prepare the reader for what is to follow? Is it clear? Is anything missing?

step 2

Rewrite your essay, making any necessary changes. Turn this revised draft of your essay in to your teacher.

CHAPTER eleven

The Physical World

in this chapter

You will collect information about environment and culture and write about how the environment affects people's lifestyles.

PART one
Ideas for Writing

Getting Started

The great variety in geographical features around the world is astounding: the high mountains of Tibet, the ice and snow of the arctic regions, the lush jungles of South America, the flat open spaces of the Middle West of the United States. Have you ever wondered what life is like for the people who live in a region that is very different from yours? What effect does geography have on the culture and history of a group of people? Do geographical differences cause cultural differences? You're going to consider these ideas in this chapter.

Study these photos of various parts of the world and their inhabitants and then answer the questions.

1. What parts of the world do these photographs represent? Match the photo numbers on the left with the place names on the right.

1.

2.

3.

4.

5.

6.

PHOTO	PLACE NAME
1.	Mekong River, Thailand
2.	Alaska
3.	Tahiti
4.	Los Angeles, California
5.	Peru
6.	Taos, New Mexico

2. How do these areas of the world differ from each other?

3. What are the unique environmental features (natural or manmade) of each one?

Brainstorming

In small groups, list all the facts you are aware of about the people who live in these parts of the world. Think about what kind of work they do, what they eat, what they wear, their type of housing, their religion, their political and social systems, their artwork, and anything else you can think of. Use the chart on the facing page. Some examples for photos 2 and 6 are given.

	location	work	food	clothing	type of housing	other
1.						
2.	Los Angeles	movie industry		western; casual	apartments	
3.						
4.						
5.						
6.	Tahiti	farming fishing	fruit fish			

Freewriting

Write for fifteen minutes without stopping about the physical environment of the area that you come from. Is it urban or rural? What geographical features are there? Mountains? Desert? Lakes? Is it near the ocean? What is the weather like? What manmade features is it known for? Tall buildings? Ancient ruins?

Reading for Ideas

The following is an excerpt from *Never in Anger: Portrait of an Eskimo Family*. The author, Jean L. Briggs, is a Canadian anthropologist who wanted to learn about Eskimo, or Inuit, culture. To do this, she made friends with an Eskimo family in the Utku tribe who agreed to let her live with them as one of the family. She became very close to her Eskimo family and even refers to the members as "my father," "my sister," and so forth. In this selection, she describes how the Utku feel about having to move frequently because of their harsh environment. Before you read the essay, answer the following questions.

prereading questions

1. In what part of the world do Inuit live? ______________________________
2. Describe the region in which they live in as much detail as you can. ______________________________
3. What do the Inuit eat? ______________________________
4. What do they wear? ______________________________
5. What is a *nomad?* ______________________________
6. What is an *igloo?* ______________________________

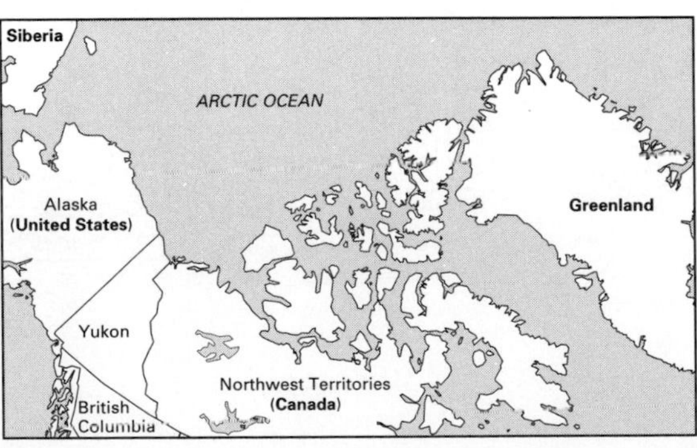

The Arctic region includes the northern timberlines of North America and Eurasia.

Never in Anger: Portrait of an Eskimo Family

Nomadic life is very pleasurable for the Utku. Difficult as moving sometimes is—when the sled runners run into snowdrifts and stick, when the river-snow becomes soaked with water so that dogs and people slosh deep in slush and are soon drenched, when winds bite at noses and toes so that the children tied atop the load cry with cold or shrink silently into the protective quilts wrapped around them—nevertheless, a move to a new campsite is a memorable break in the ordinary flow of life. People look forward to the change of season. In the autumn, the talk is about how good it will feel to move into an igloo. The night before we set off for Amujat,* my first October at Black River, Inuttiaq, my Eskimo father, lying in bed, gestured in the air the motions of cutting snow blocks and sang a little song about tomorrow's igloo building. In the spring, when the igloos have been transformed by long occupancy into small caves of dirty grey ice, the talk turns to the pleasures of the spring moves: "Igloos are unpleasant in the spring," they say. "The water of Amujat tastes unpleasantly of salt; it will be good to go to Itimnaaqjuk* and fish." And people pantomime the motions of fishing for trout through the ice.

Even the process of moving holds excitement. A happy bustle of activity pervades a camp that is preparing to move. Packing is done at a double-quick tempo, orders given and obeyed with an energy rarely seen in the quiet life of a settled camp. In the spring, when thawing weather and the search for fish required frequent moves, the spirit of impermanence seemed to infect people, so that, from my point of view, they seemed to make the maximum rather than the minimum necessary number of moves. At this season, unlike any other, tents were shifted for the slightest reason: because the gravel floor had become soiled with bits of paper and fishbones, or because a change in the wind was filling the tent with mosquitoes. Shifting was not done for such small reasons in the more permanent summer camp; there, the unwanted foreign matter was picked out of the gravel and the mosquitoes were simply endured. In spring, too, when the flooding river forced us uphill, the retreat was always made foot by foot as the river rose. For several days we moved camp at least once a day and sometimes more often, and always when the water had arrived within inches of our doorsteps. Once as we were setting up the tents for the third or fourth time, I asked the friend who was helping me: "Does the water

---

**Amujat, Itimnaaqjuk* Names of places in the region

come up this high?" (I indicated the spot where we were placing the tents.) "Sometimes it does and sometimes it doesn't," was the answer.

I do not know what made people move this way. It may have been optimism; weakened by measles, as the Utku were that spring, they may have hoped that each small move would be the last. But then why shift the tent to escape the mosquitoes or improve the flooring? It sometimes seemed as though rearranging the environment by moving were a form of play for the Eskimos, a pleasure in itself. Whatever the explanation, I never completely shared the Eskimo spirit. I found it a trying job to pull up a tent, move all its contents uphill in my arms, set up the tent again and rearrange the interior. Once it was done, I enjoyed the freshness of a new home, a tent floor carpeted with reindeer moss and cranberry blossoms.* Still, moves were a nuisance that upset my work and, worse, made me feel disoriented in my environment. So, in moving away from the rising water, if I could have done what I wanted, I would have moved, once and for all, the few hundred feet to the top of the hill and sat there securely, looking down at the flood.

The fact that the moves were always made with no time to spare I sometimes found a little disturbing, too. I was never quite sure when I went to bed with the water two feet from my door whether I was going to wake up floating. One such evening I remarked to Inuttiaq that the dogs, who were chained to boulders at the water's edge, were going to get wet during the night. "Yes, they are," he said. And sure enough, in the morning several dogs were standing belly-deep in the flood, their noses pointing stiffly skyward.

In the course of many years of moving up and down the river, from campsite to campsite, from one fishing place to another, the countryside that seemed so limitless to me and at first sight so empty, had become to its inhabitants as marked with familiar associations as a friend's face. It may be partly the recognition of these landmarks together with the excitement of change that gives the Utku pleasure in their way of life. Like other wandering people, the Utku have a remarkable memory for the details of their territory, and the accuracy with which they observe and mentally record the shape of the terrain and their skill in making and reading maps are phenomenal. I showed several Utku men maps of the entire North American Arctic. They pointed out and named correctly all the major rivers, lakes, and islands in a territory approximately 135,000 miles square.

Jean L. Briggs

**Reindeer moss, cranberry blossoms* Plants found in this region

postreading questions

1. Describe the Utkus' attitude toward their nomadic lifestyle.

2. Does the author know *why* the Utkus feel the way they do about moving?

3. Why do the Utkus move from their igloos in the spring?

4. Why else do the Utkus move from place to place?

5. Describe the Utkus' relationship with their territory.

6. What didn't the author like about moving? Why do you think she felt this way?

7. Would you enjoy a nomadic lifestyle? Why? Why not?

8. Name some other nomadic groups in the world.

Gathering Information

A *scavenger hunt* is a game in which the players, in teams, must find unusual objects or answers to difficult questions. The team that finishes first and has the most correct items wins. The following is a scavenger hunt in which you find answers to difficult questions about how environment affects the cultures of the world.

Divide into small groups. Try to be the first group to have all correct answers to the following questions. You may interview classmates, friends, professors at your school, or others, and you may do library research. You will notice that some of the following questions are more difficult than others, and some of them are actually groups of questions on the same topic. Answer the questions by working with other students in your group.

1. Name an ethnic group noted for longevity (having a long life). How is this longevity influenced by the environment in which these people live?

   ____

   ____

   ____

2. How many words for *snow* do Eskimos have?

   ____

   ____

3. What does manifest destiny mean? What does it have to do with American history and/or culture?

   ____

   ____

   ____

4. How many uses did the American Plains Indians have for the buffalo? What were they? ______________________________

   ____

   ____

5. Which five cities have the greatest population density? How did these cities become so large? ______________________________

   ____

   ____

   ____

   ____

   ____

6. Which five countries in the world have the largest populations? For each country, find out how many languages are spoken.

7. Find one religion in which a natural phenomenon (a mountain, the sea, and so forth) plays an important part. Explain the significance of this phenomenon in the religion.

8. What are the five longest rivers in the world? Choose three and explain how the rivers affect life in these areas.

9. Briefly describe the attitudes and lifestyles of people who live in the Hawaiian Islands. Consider both the native Polynesians and the Asians, Americans, and Europeans who have settled there. How does their geographical setting influence their behavior?

10. Which area of the world has the greatest rainfall? The least? How do these conditions affect the people who live in these areas?

THINKING CRITICALLY

Building on Your Knowledge Base

When answering a question or gathering information, consider first what you already know about the subject. Building on your knowledge base will give you more confidence when approaching an academic task.

Jot down some facts you know about the geographical areas listed below:

Saudi Arabia ____________________

Mediterranean Sea ____________________

Istanbul ____________________

East Germany ____________________

Trinidad ____________________

Tahiti ____________________

Southwestern United States ____________________

Afghanistan ____________________

Haiti ____________________

PART two
Language for Writing

Describing Environmental Conditions

Look at each of the environmental terms in the pictures on page 229. Write all the words and expressions that come into your mind as you see each term by making a vocabulary diagram like the one shown in the example. Write down anything that you think of, but make sure that what you write is related to the original term. Notice that you can use nouns, verbs, adjectives, or other expressions.

example:

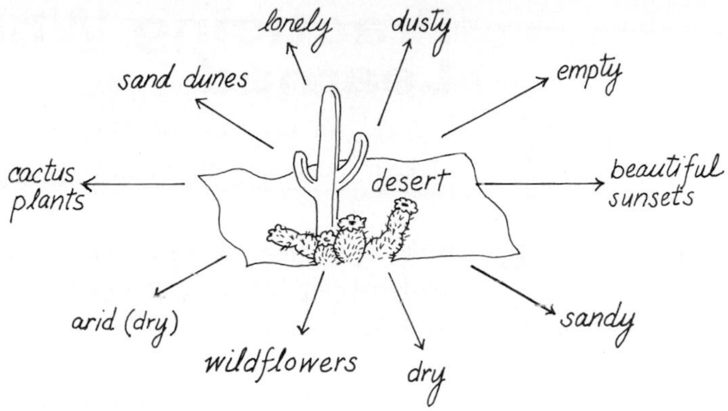

Now make a list of the new words. Divide them into nouns, verbs, adjectives, and expressions, as we have done in previous chapters. Share your list with your classmates.

Practicing What You've Learned

Make a vocabulary diagram for the Arctic region.

Write a paragraph in which you describe one of your favorite places (indoors or outdoors). Include descriptions of any people, animals, plants, or objects that you see there.

Choose one of the vocabulary diagrams you made and use the words in it to write a paragraph about that region (mountains, arctic region, valley, etc.) Try to use the kind of descriptive language that Briggs uses in "Never in Anger" on pages 223 and 224.

Write another paragraph in which you discuss one of the regions of the world shown in the photographs in Part One. Use the vocabulary from this section and consider the inhabitants of the region and how their environment influences their attitudes and lifestyles.

PART three
Systems for Writing

Review Points

- Well-developed paragraphs discuss information in detail.
- These details help answer the questions a reader may have.

Using Sensory Details

New Points

- Sensory details allow readers to see, hear and feel things just as the author saw, heard, and felt them.
- Writers use sensory details to develop their paragraphs and make them more descriptive.

"Never in Anger" provides a good picture of the environment and lifestyle of the Inuit because the author uses sensory details to make it descriptive. The sensory details in the following paragraph from the article are underlined. Read the paragraph and answer the questions that follow.

> Nomadic life is very pleasurable for the Utku. Difficult as moving sometimes is—when the sled runners run into snowdrifts and stick, when the river-snow becomes soaked with water so that dogs and people slosh deep in slush and are soon drenched, when winds bite at noses and toes so that the children tied atop the load cry with cold or shrink silently into the protective quilts wrapped around them—nevertheless, a move to a new campsite is a memorable break in the ordinary flow of life.

Which words and phrases help you see things clearly? Hear things? Feel things?

Now read another passage. This time, find and underline the descriptive words and phrases. This passage contains language that helps you *taste* things, as well.

> The night before we set off for Amujat, my first October at Black River, Inuttiaq, my Eskimo father, lying in bed, gestured in the air motions of cutting snow blocks and sang a little song about tomorrow's igloo building. In the spring, when the igloos have been transformed by long occupancy into small caves of dirty grey ice, the talk turns to the pleasures of the spring moves: "Igloos are unpleasant in the spring," they say. "The water of Amujat tastes unpleasantly of salt; it will be good to go to Itimnaaqjuk and fish." And people pantomine the motions of fishing for trout through the ice.

The following paragraph does not contain many specific details. Read the paragraph. Then, with a partner, make a list of questions about what you feel the author has left out. Write at least one question for each numbered sentence. They can be either yes/no or information questions (see Part Three, Chapter Seven for examples). Think about sensory details that are missing as well as any other kinds of information.

> (1) I used to live in Hawaii. (2) I had a job there, but I didn't have to work very hard. (3) I went to one of the most beautiful beaches in the world every day after work. (4) The weather was always nice in Hawaii, so I wore shorts and sandals everywhere. (5) On the weekends, I went fishing with my Hawaiian friend. (6) We often ate what we caught, along with other native Hawaiian dishes that my friend's mother would prepare. (7) How I miss my life in Paradise!

Some of your questions may be:

1. What is Hawaii like?
2. What was his job? In what way was his job easy?
3. What does the most beautiful beach in the world look like? What kinds of things did he do there? What did the ocean waves sound like? What did the sand feel like under his bare feet?
4. Tell me more about the weather: Was it always sunny? Were there breezes? Did the air smell good?
5. What was his friend like?
6. What were some of the native dishes they prepared? What did they taste like?

To answer all these questions, the author would have to write much more than one paragraph. But by asking just a few of these questions, then supplying a few more specific, sensory details, the writer would be prepared to write a more interesting paragraph and a better developed essay.

focus on testing

Adding Specific Details

When taking a timed writing test, writers can forget to include important facts. When writing under a time limit, remember to ask and answer questions to help you include specific details in your essay. The details will make your essay more interesting, persuasive, and complete.

Practicing What You've Learned

Write a "bare-bones" paragraph about your favorite vacation place. Think about a place that is very different from where you live. It can either be a place you have actually been to or one that you would like to visit. Write four or five sentences. Exchange paragraphs with a partner and make a list of questions for each other. Discuss your answers with your partner. Rewrite your paragraph, filling in the details. Exchange paragraphs again. See if your questions were answered.

Bring a picture of an interesting part of the world to class. You might find one in a magazine such as *National Geographic* or in a travel brochure from a travel agency. Make a list of questions about what you would like to know about this place. See if anyone in the class has been there and can answer your questions. Have the person give as many sensory details as possible. Take notes, then use the information in one or two well-developed paragraphs about the picture.

Writing Assignments

Write an essay on one of the following topics. Use new vocabulary and expressions you learned in this chapter and make sure that your paragraphs are clear and coherent. Develop your ideas by using information from the research you did in Part One.

1. Discuss the effects of the environmental features of a particular part of the world on the people who live there. Use the information you gathered in Part One.
2. Compare two different regions of the world. In your comparison, consider the environmental features and how they affect the inhabitants.
3. Answer one of the following questions:
   Why do people who live in warm climates tend to be more relaxed?
   What are some of the effects of living in a crowded urban area?
   What effect does environment have on the longevity of a group of people?
4. Take one of the paragraphs you wrote and turn it into an essay.
5. Agree with, disagree with, or explain the following quotation:

   "There is no solitude in the world like that of the big city." —*Kathleen Norris*

6. Write an essay about any aspect of environment and culture that interests you.

PART four

Evaluating for Rewriting

Working with Your Partner

Exchange the essays you wrote for the Writing Assignments section. Use the following questionnaire to evaluate each other's essays.

1. Look at the first paragraph of the body. Is it adequately *developed?*

   Yes _____ No _____

   If not, what are some of the questions you have about the ideas that the author has not answered?

Are there enough details in the paragraph? List them. If there aren't enough, make suggestions.

____

____

____

Do you have any general comments about the way the ideas in this paragraph were developed?

2. Look at the second paragraph of the body. Is it adequately *developed*?

   Yes _____ No _____

   If not, what are some of the questions you have about the ideas that the author has not answered?

   Are there enough details in the paragraph? List them. If there aren't enough, make suggestions.

   ____

   ____

   ____

   Do you have any general comments about the way the ideas in this paragraph were developed?

3. Look at the third paragraph of the body. Is it adequately *developed*?

   Yes _____ No _____

   If not, what are some of the questions you have about the ideas that the author has not answered?

   Are there enough details in the paragraph? List them. If there aren't enough, make suggestions.

   ____

   ____

   ____

   Do you have any general comments about the way the ideas in this paragraph were developed?

   ____

   ____

   ____

   ____

   ____

   ____

Return each other's essays. Read your partner's evaluation of your essay. Discuss any questions you have with your partner.

Working on Your Own

Now you should be ready to evaluate your own paper. Go through the questions again. Take into consideration what your partner said about your essay when he or she evaluated it. Are there unclear elements? Is anything missing? Is there more to say? Words to change?

Rewrite your essay, making any necessary changes. Turn this revised draft of your essay in to your teacher.

CHAPTER twelve

Together on a Small Planet

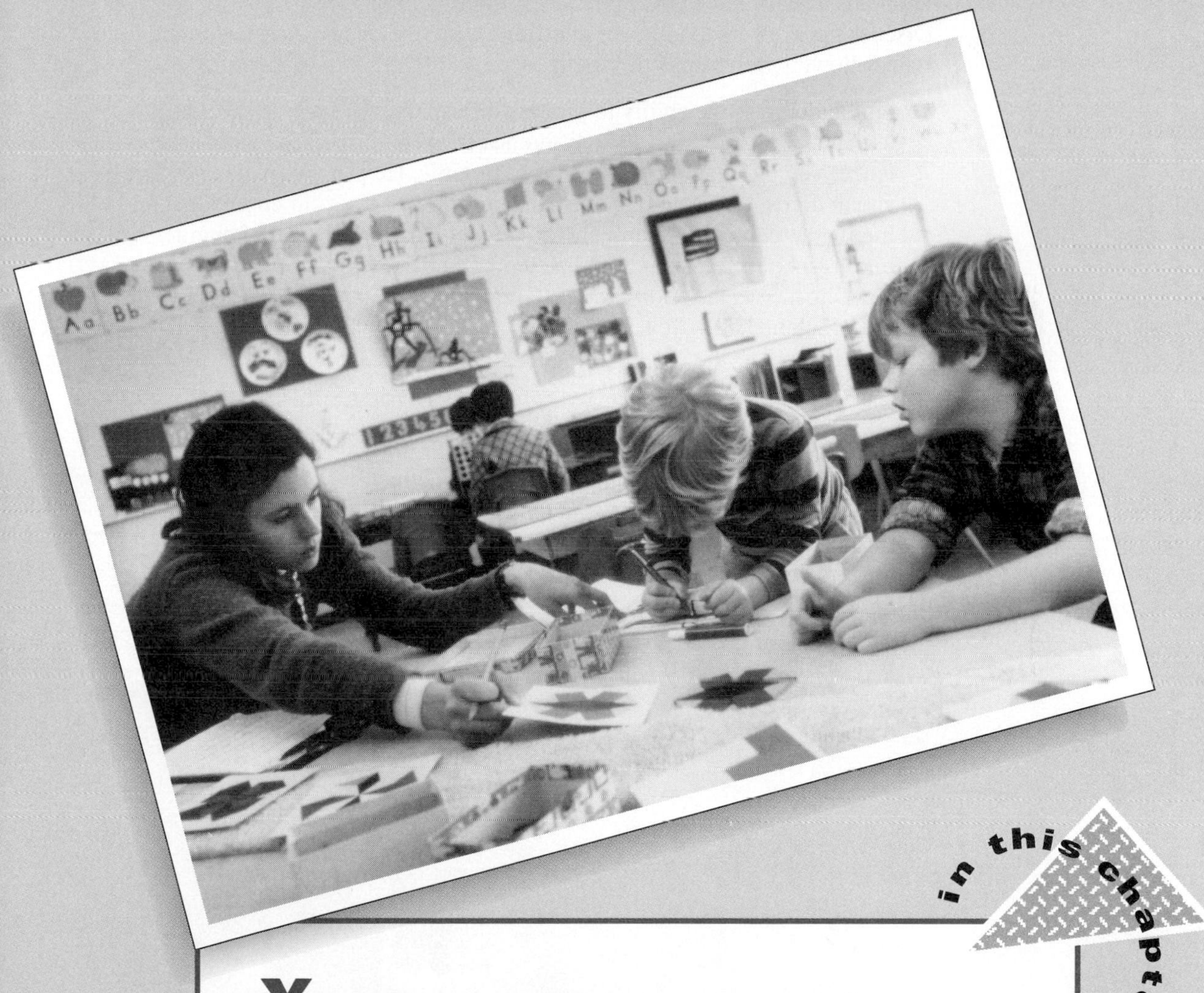

in this chapter

You will do research on a person famous for brilliant thinking and write about an aspect of intelligence that interests you.

PART one
Ideas for Writing

Getting Started

Think about your definition of intelligence for a moment. Does your culture determine your definition? How do we use intelligence in our everyday lives? Have we used our intelligence to create the world we live in? Think of examples that show how humans have or have not applied their intelligence.

Discuss the answers to all these questions with one or two classmates and then read the following definitions of intelligence.

1. "Intelligence is the ability to process information in such a way that it is useful in your life. There's a difference between intelligence and competence. The intelligent person is more flexible. He can apply his knowledge and abilities. For example, one can learn how to fix a car engine, but an intelligent person can apply those concepts to another type of engine. An intelligent person can extrapolate to another field." *—Lucia Blakeslee*
2. "Intelligence is the ability to grasp new information quickly and put it to use efficiently." *—Nancy Vankat*
3. "Intelligence is the capacity to do well on an intelligence test." *—Edwin Boring*
4. "Intelligence unites us with mankind, by leading us in sympathy to other times, other places, other customs." *—John Erskine*
5. "If an animal does something, they call it instinct. If we do exactly the same thing for the same reason, they call it intelligence. I guess what they mean is that we all make mistakes, but intelligence enables us to do it on purpose." *—Will Cuppy*
6. "Intellect distinguishes between the possible and the impossible; reason distinguishes between the sensible and the senseless. Even the possible can be senseless." *—Max Born*

Brainstorming

With a partner, make a list of as many things as you can think of that contribute to intelligence. Use your imagination.

____

____

____

____

____

____

____

Freewriting

What do *you* think intelligence is? Do you agree with any of the definitions at the beginning of this section? Or do you have a completely different definition? Write for fifteen minutes on your personal definition of intelligence. As you write, consider the questions you discussed with your classmates at the beginning of this chapter.

Reading for Ideas

You are going to read an essay by Mark Twain (1835–1910), one of America's greatest humorists. He wrote this essay approximately 100 years ago, so some references to people and places of his time have been omitted. Still, you will be able to understand some of Twain's subtle humor. Read the selection quickly and do not be concerned with understanding all the ideas and vocabulary. Before you read "The Lowest Animal," answer the following questions.

prereading questions

1. What do you think distinguishes humans from animals?

____

____

2. Are certain animals intelligent? Which ones? How are they intelligent?

____

____

3. Do you think humans are more intelligent than animals? Explain your answer.

____

____

4. Can intelligence be measured? How?

____

____

5. Are there cultural differences in the way we define intelligence? Explain your answer.

____

____

6. Discuss the meaning of these words before you read: trait, renounce, earl, anaconda, avaricious.

____

____

The Lowest Animal

I have been studying the traits and dispositions of the "lower animals" (so-called), and contrasting them with the traits and dispositions of man. I find the result humiliating to me. For it obliges me to renounce my allegiance to the Darwinian Theory of the Ascent of Man from the Lower Animals; since it now seems plain to me that the theory ought to be vacated in favor of a new and truer one, this new and truer one to be named the Descent of Man from the Higher Animals.

In proceeding toward this unpleasant conclusion I have not guessed or speculated or conjectured, but have used what is commonly called the scientific method. Some of my experiments were quite curious. In the course of my reading I had come across a case where, many years ago, some hunters on our Great Plains organized a buffalo hunt for the entertainment of an English earl—that, and to provide some fresh meat. They killed seventy-two of those great animals; and ate part of one of them and left the seventy-one to rot. In order to determine the difference between an anaconda and an earl—if any—I caused seven young calves to be turned into the anaconda's cage. The grateful reptile immediately crushed one of them and swallowed it, then lay back satisfied. It showed no further interest in the calves, and no disposition to harm them. I tried this experiment with other anacondas; always with the same result. The fact stood proven that the difference between an earl and an anaconda is that the earl is cruel and the anaconda isn't; and that the earl wantonly destroys what he has no use for, but the anaconda doesn't. This seemed to suggest that the anaconda was not descended from the earl. It also seemed to suggest that the earl was descended from the anaconda, and had lost a good deal in the transition.

I furnished a hundred different kinds of wild and tame animals the opportunity to accumulate vast stores of food, but none of them would do it. The squirrels and bees and certain birds made accumulations, but stopped when they had gathered a winter's supply, and could not be persuaded to add to it. In order to bolster up a tottering reputation the ant pretended to store up supplies, but I was not deceived. I know the ant. These experiments convinced me that there is this difference between man and the higher animals: he is avaricious and miserly, they are not.

In the course of my experiments I convinced myself that among the animals man is the only one that harbors insults and injuries, broods over them, waits till a chance offers, then takes revenge. The passion of revenge is unknown to the higher animals.

Roosters keep harems, but it is by consent of their concubines; therefore no wrong is done. Men keep harems, but it is by brute force, privileged by atrocious laws which the other sex is allowed no hand in making. In this matter man occupies a far lower place than the rooster.

Indecency, vulgarity, obscenity—these are strictly confined to man; he invented them. Among the higher animals there is no trace of them. Of all the animals, man is the only one that is cruel. He is the only one that inflicts pain for the pleasure of doing it. It is a trait that is not known to the higher animals. The cat plays with the frightened mouse; but she has this excuse, that she does not know that the mouse is suffering. The cat is moderate—unhumanly moderate: she only scares the mouse; she does not hurt it; she doesn't dig out its eyes, or tear off its skin, or drive splinters under its nails—man-fashion; when she is done playing with it she makes a sudden meal of it and puts it out of its trouble. Man is the Cruel Animal. He is alone in that distinction.

The higher animals engage in individual fights, but never in organized masses. Man is the only animal that deals in that atrocity of atrocities, War. Man is the only animal that robs his helpless fellow of his country—takes possession of it and drives him out of it or destroys him. Man has done this in all the ages. There is not an acre of ground on the globe that is in possession of its rightful owner, or that has not been taken away from owner after owner, cycle after cycle, by force and bloodshed.

Man is the only Slave. And he is the only animal who enslaves. He has always been a slave in one form or another, and has always held other slaves in bondage under him in one way or another. In our day he is always some man's slave for wages, and does that man's work; and this slave has other slaves under him for minor wages, and they do *his* work. The higher animals are the only ones who exclusively do their own work and provide their own living.

Man is the Reasoning Animal. Such is the claim. I think it is open to dispute. Indeed, my experiments have proven to me that he is the Unreasoning Animal. Note his history, as sketched above. It seems plain to me that whatever he is he is *not* a reasoning animal. His record is the fantastic record of a maniac. In truth, man in incurably foolish. Simple things which the other animals easily learn, he is incapable of learning.

And so I find that we have descended and degenerated, from some far ancestor—some microscopic atom wandering at its pleasure between the mighty horizons of a drop of water perchance—insect by insect, animal by animal, reptile by reptile, down the long highway of smirchless innocence, till we have reached the bottom stages of development—namable as the Human Being. Below us—nothing.

Mark Twain

1. According to Twain, what should we rename Darwin's theory of the Ascent of Man?

2. What is the scientific method? Share what you know about it with your classmates.

3. What does Twain mean when he refers to higher animals and lower animals?

4. What does the material Twain read about the Great Plains hunters show him? What are his conclusions about the differences between an anaconda and an earl?

5. Record some of Twain's conclusions in the chart below. Add some categories of your own.

category	what some animals do	what people do
wastefulness		
greed		
revengefulness		

6. According to Twain, which is the "Lowest Animal?"

7. Do you agree with Twain? How would you respond to what he has written?

8. Do you think Twain really performed these experiments? Was he being serious when he wrote "The Lowest Animal?" Look for instances of humor in his writing.

9. Pretend you are Mark Twain. Based on what you've read, write a paragraph explaining "your" definition of intelligence.

THINKING CRITICALLY

Recognizing Date Clues

When you analyze a piece of writing, it's useful to keep in mind the time period in which it was created. Although Twain wrote "The Lowest Animal" 100 years ago, some readers might say it describes conditions today. In small groups, review the selection and look for language or references that "date" the piece (that is, which make it obvious that it was written in the last century). Put a "d" next to these parts. Then look for language or references that seem contemporary (modern). Indicate these with a "c."

Gathering Information

Whom do you consider to be very intelligent? Choose a well-known figure (past or present) famous for brilliant thinking and find out as much as you can about him or her. Do his or her qualities match any of those described by the definitions of intelligence in the first section? Choose someone from any field, in any country.

You might choose a philosopher, a scientist, a writer, a teacher, an inventor, or a mechanic. Write a paragraph on why you (and others) consider this person intelligent.

PART two

Language for Writing

Discussing Intelligence

The definitions of intelligence in the quotations in Part One may have included language that is new to you. This exercise will help you understand this language for defining intelligence so you can use it in writing or speaking.

The following is a list of some useful words and expressions. Make sure you understand each one. The first one is done as an example. Then give an accurate synonym or synonymous expression for each in the following chart. Be sure to find synonyms that relate to the topic of intelligence by examining how the words and expressions listed are used in the quotations on page 238. At the end of the chart, write any additional words or expressions that you find useful in discussing intelligence.

words and expressions	synonyms
to process information	to make sense of (to understand) information
competence	
to extrapolate	
to grasp new information	
capacity	
instinct	
to do something on purpose	
intellect	
reason	

Writing Definitions

Sometimes writers want to define a word or expression. There are two types of definitions: *literal* and *stipulative.* A literal definition is one that is commonly accepted and can be found in a dictionary. A stipulated definition is more limited and subjective. It can be an interpretation of a word or a simplification of a term.

Review the following list of words and expressions that are useful when writing definitions. Then see how they are used in the examples.

WORDS AND EXPRESSIONS FOR DEFINING

X (word or expression) { is . . . / means . . . / denotes . . . / reflects . . . / indicates . . . / can be interpreted as . . .

is { understood / considered / believed } to be . . .

Examples:

1. Intelligence is the ability to grasp new information quickly and put it to use efficiently.
2. In Chinese families, *shau* means respect for one's parents shown through actions.
3. The word *deadline* denotes a definite time limit for completion of a task; no such word exists in some languages, like Spanish.
4. *Salaam* in Arabic can be interpreted as either "hello" or "goodbye."

Practicing What You've Learned

exercise 1 Write a paragraph about the person you researched in Part One. Be sure to include why you consider this person to be intelligent and what you mean by *intelligence*.

exercise 2 Choose one of the following words and explain what you think it means.

love	sympathy
honor	patience
respect	duty

exercise 3 Write a response to Twain's essay on page 240 to 242 in which you discuss your definition of intelligence.

PART three
Systems for Writing

Review Points

- When you write a well-developed paragraph, you put all your ideas in a logical order.
- The way you order your ideas in a paragraph depends on the topic you are discussing.

Essay Organization

New Points

- To write a well-organized essay, put clearly developed paragraphs into an order that is coherent and easy for the reader to follow.
- You can establish this order with your thesis statement: It acts as a preview for the reader, preparing her or him for what is to follow.
- If you keep your thesis statement in mind as you write, you'll end up with a well-organized essay.

Read this thesis statement and answer the questions that follow.

> Being aware of cross-cultural differences in nonverbal behavior makes communication with people from different backgrounds more effective.

1. What is the main idea?

____

____

____

2. What are the supporting ideas?

____

____

____

3. How will the essay be organized?

____

____

____

One way to organize an essay based on this thesis would be to present one reason for the main idea in each paragraph. An outline for this essay might look like this:

I. Paragraph 1: Introduction and thesis statement
II. Paragraph 2: Knowledge about nonverbal behavior helps one avoid misunderstandings.
III. Paragraph 3: An awareness of nonverbal behavior helps one develop a deeper appreciation of other cultures.
IV. Paragraph 4: Knowing about differences in nonverbal behavior helps one communicate more effectively.
V. Paragraph 5: Conclusion

Another way to organize an essay based on the same thesis statement would be to describe people who do and don't know about cross-cultural differences and show the results of their knowledge (or lack of knowledge) to convince the reader of your point. An outline for this essay would look like this:

I. Paragraph 1: Introduction and thesis statement
II. Paragraph 2: People who are not aware of cross-cultural differences in nonverbal behavior can have difficulty communicating and being understood.
III. Paragraph 3: People who understand cross-cultural differences can establish friendships and learn more about their international acquaintances through an increased ability to communicate.
IV. Paragraph 4: Conclusion

Three Essay Organization Patterns

New Points

There are three easy-to-remember organization patterns for three common essay types:

- Showing cause and effect
- Comparing two things
- Showing advantages and disadvantages

Take a look at these three basic organization systems:

SYSTEM A: SHOWING CAUSE AND EFFECT

First paragraph: There are three causes/effects of X: a, b, and c.
Second paragraph: All about X and a
Third paragraph: All about X and b
Fourth paragraph: All about X and c
Fifth paragraph: Conclusion

SYSTEM B: COMPARING TWO THINGS

First paragraph: X is similar to (different from) Y in three areas: a, b, and c.
Second paragraph: All about X and Y in light of a
Third paragraph: All about X and Y in light of b
Fourth paragraph: All about X and Y in light of c
Fifth paragraph: Conclusion

SYSTEM C: SHOWING ADVANTAGES AND/OR DISADVANTAGES

First paragraph: X has three (dis)advantages: 1, 2, and 3.
Second paragraph: All about the first (dis)advantage
Third paragraph: All about the second (dis)advantage
Fourth paragraph: All about the third (dis)advantage
Fifth paragraph: Conclusion

Practicing What You've Learned

Read the following thesis statements and describe how you think the essays they introduce are going to be organized. First, decide what the main idea is and then determine the supporting points. Take note of the *order* in which the supporting ideas are presented. Then, make outlines like the preceding ones to show the possible organization of an essay.

1. The gestures people use in the United States and Canada when greeting family members, insulting others, and showing respect for superiors are different from those used in the Middle East.

2. Learning to write has influenced me in three ways: I think more clearly, I have more self-discipline, and I am able to concentrate better.

3. There are three advantages to the traditional grading system: it motivates students to work harder, it provides a standardized measure of student achievement, and it is objective rather than subjective.

4. Although they are very different, both physical and mental leisure-time activities have benefits that are stimulating and constructive.

5. Both travel and study in a foreign country result in intellectual and emotional growth.

6. It is important to learn the nonverbal language of a new culture in order to communicate effectively in that culture and to have a complete understanding of it.

exercise 2

This exercise is similar to Exercise 1, but the thesis statements here are less prescriptive and more open to different types of development than the thesis statements in the previous exercise. Outline each of them as thoroughly as you can, then compare your outlines with a classmate's. Discuss which plans are more efficient, more convincing, and more coherent.

1. Because of the dramatically different role of religion in the two cultures, life in the United States and in the Middle East is very different.

2. It is essential for people in science and technology to know and be able to use the English language correctly.

3. Intelligence is not only knowledge—it is also common sense.

4. Success is the ability to do what you want to do and to be satisfied with yourself.

focus on testing

Basing Your Essay on Your Thesis Statement

Exercises 1 and 2 on pages 249 to 253 ask you to analyze some thesis statements and then write possible outlines for the essays they introduce. These exercises show the relationship between the thesis statement and the organization of the essay itself. When taking an essay test, you can save valuable time if you keep this relationship in mind. Accordingly, write a thesis statement that has clearly distinguished supporting points. Use the order of the supporting points to organize your essay. Paraphrase your supporting points to make them the topic sentences for the body paragraphs of your essay.

Your teacher is going to assign one of the essays in the following Writing Assignments section (or ask you to choose one). Before you actually start to write, complete the following steps.

Step 1. Study the essay assignment carefully. Then write your thesis statement for it. Do some prewriting activities to get started, such as jotting down ideas about the topic.

Step 2. Before you write the essay itself, exchange your thesis statement with a partner and see if he or she can determine an organizational pattern for you, based solely on the thesis statement. If this is too difficult, the thesis probably isn't complete enough. Rewrite it. If it's easy, congratulations—you probably have a good thesis.

Step 3. If your partner determines an organizational pattern for your essay, take back your thesis statement and, on the same piece of paper, briefly outline the essay you intend to write. The outline should include your thesis, the topic sentences of all your paragraphs, and brief descriptions of the examples or explanations you intend to use to develop each paragraph.

Step 4. Give the thesis and outline to your teacher and have him or her check your organization and ideas at this point, to see if you're on the right track. Your teacher may ask you to rethink your outline or may tell you to go ahead and write your first draft.

Writing Assignments

Write an essay on one of the following topics. Use new vocabulary and expressions you learned in this chapter and make sure that your paragraphs are clear and coherent. Develop your ideas by using information from the research you did in Part One.

1. Compare two different views on what intelligence is. Use the information you gathered in Part One. Cite authorities in your essay.
2. Discuss the effects of superior intelligence on an individual's daily life. Use the information you gathered in Part One. Try to incorporate the paragraph you wrote in Part One into your essay.
3. Summarize and react to Twain's essay "The Lowest Animal" on pages 240 to 242.
4. Write a summary of and react to one of the articles you read when you did your research for Part One.
5. What is the best way to measure intelligence?
6. Agree with, disagree with, or explain the following quote:

   "Genius is 2 percent inspiration and 98 percent perspiration." —*Thomas Edison*

7. Write an essay on any aspect of intelligence that interests you.

PART four

Evaluating for Rewriting

Working with Your Partner

With a partner, make your own evaluation questionnaire for the previous essay. Your questionnaire should include questions about all the important points you've learned about writing since you began this course. You may want to skim through each chapter for ideas. Make sure you include questions on the thesis statement, topic sentences, paragraph development and organization, and introductions and conclusions. Write your questions in the following space.

1. ____________________

   ____

2. ____________________

   ____

3. ____________________

   ____

4. ____________________

   ____

5. ______________________________

____

6. ______________________________

____

7. ______________________________

____

8. ______________________________

____

9. ______________________________

____

10. ______________________________

____

step 2 Exchange the essays you wrote for the Writing Assignments section. Use your questionnaire to evaluate each other's essays.

step 3 Return each other's essays. Read your partner's evaluation of your essay. Discuss any questions you have with your partner.

Working on Your Own

step 1 Using the questionnaire, answer the questions about your own essay. Consider these answers and your partner's evaluation comments before you rewrite your essay.

step 2 Rewrite your essay, making any necessary changes. Turn this revised draft of your essay in to your teacher.

Answers to Selected Exercises and Questions

CHAPTER one

pp. 2–3 Suggested photo captions (many interpretations are possible):

2. Food: Time is valuable, so Americans often eat on the run/in a hurry/while they are doing something else.
3. Family: There is no "typical" American family./Although the American family is changing, most parents want a good life for their children.
4. Work: Americans value hard work./Americans change jobs frequently.
5. Education: Many Americans value informality, even in education.
6. Health and fitness: Many Americans are health conscious.

p. 7 Thinking Critically

1a. He can't—can be inferred.
1b. Cannot be inferred.
1c. He did—can be inferred.
1d. Cannot be inferred.

pp. 9–10 Asking Information Questions. Sample questions:

What kinds of problems did you encounter when you first came here?
When did you arrive?
Where did you find a place to live?
How much trouble did you have with the language at first?
How many friends have you made here?
How long do you plan to stay here?
Why did you decide to study in the United States/Canada?

pp. 14–19

Exercise 1: In all three paragraphs, the topic sentence is the first sentence.
Exercise 2: A: 3; **B:** 2; **C:** 1
Exercise 3: Sample predictions (several interpretations are possible):

1. The paragraph probably will relate a humorous anecdote about a cross-cultural misunderstanding in a restaurant, e.g., ordering the wrong thing, table/restaurant manners.
2. This paragraph probably will be a personal narrative by someone living in a new culture about the positive and negative experiences she or he had; e.g., a positive experience may be discovering new ways of doing things, and a negative experience may be loneliness.
3. This paragraph probably is about the problems a newcomer encounters and how the absence of family and friends makes life more difficult, e.g., when making important decisions for which the family is often consulted (such as what to study, making a major purchase, getting married).

Exercise 4: Suggestions for topic sentences:

A. Nonverbal communication in North America is very different from nonverbal communication in South America.
B. Americans are easy to spot no matter where they are.
C. All cultures have specific gestures for greeting and leave taking.

CHAPTER two

pp. 26–27 Getting Started. Possible opposing viewpoints for each argument (additional ways of expressing them are in pp. 28–29 in the Brainstorming section):

1. Lecture classes are better.
2. It is important to get a good education first.
3. You should go to college to prepare yourself for future work.
4. Studying many subjects broadens your knowledge and gives you more options for future work.
5. I majored in science to get more in-depth preparation in a specialized field.
6. Many students prefer a teacher who is more of an authority figure because it makes them feel confident that the teacher really knows his or her subject matter.
7. Continued emphasis on European ideas and history is important because it maintains traditional educational standards.
8. A competitive atmosphere stimulates learning and makes people work harder.

p. 33 Thinking Critically. Possible answers:

Advantages: College will help you earn more money/become a better person/learn to be a responsible citizen/prepare for meaningful work/learn to get along with others/practice social skills.
Disadvantages: College doesn't necessarily prepare you for your chosen profession because there aren't enough good jobs to go around/you learn a lot of things that aren't useful in your job.

pp. 40–43

Exercise 1: Paragraph **A:** Eliminate sentence 5. Paragraph **B:** Eliminate sentences 4 and 6. Paragraph **C:** Eliminate sentence 5.
Exercise 2: Paragraph **A:** Good. Paragraph **B:** Bad. Paragraph **C:** Good.
Exercise 3: Paragraph **B** is missing the restatement.

CHAPTER **three**

p. 55 Thinking Critically. A few possible answers:

When Audrey was a child: Her mother raised the children without much parenting help from her father. Her mother did most of the housework. Her father didn't cook.
When Audrey was a parent: She shared parenting with her husband. Her children helped with housework. Her husband did a lot of the cooking.

p. 59

Exercise 1: 1. c; 2. b; 3. c; 4. c; 5. a

p. 61 From Paragraph to Essay

1. Being a big sister has its advantages.
2. Get special treatment; have learned to be responsible and dependable; am prepared for my own family and future.
3. Same answer as for 2; i.e., each reason the writer gives to support her main idea could be developed to expand the paragraph into an essay.

pp. 64–65

Exercise 2

1. The thesis statement is similar to the topic sentence of the paragraph. The main ideas of the body paragraphs are similar to the three examples in the paragraph.
2. Details and examples.
3. In the body paragraphs.
4. All.
5. To develop the main ideas into complete paragraphs.

p. 66

Exercise 3

Topic sentence: My parents played an important role in my educational development by helping me in both material and spiritual ways . . .
Idea 1: They raised my older brothers and sisters in such a way that they would set a good example for me . . .
Idea 2: They bought me books to help me become a good student . . .
Idea 3: They took me on vacations and museum trips to enlarge my perspective . . .
Idea 4: They looked carefully at my exam results to motivate me . . .

CHAPTER **four**

p. 78 Thinking Critically. Possible answers/things to consider when analyzing Williams' study:

- All the lawyers were male; therefore, results may not apply to everyone.
- Certain professions may be more stressful than others, and participants all with the same (possibly stressful) profession may show more uniform results than a mixed group.

p. 81

Exercise 1: one possible solution:

a nonhostile personality	=	normal blood pressure
a good diet	=	a healthy heart
overeating	=	excess weight
exercise	=	strong muscles
anger	=	heart disease
smoking	=	lung cancer
relaxing	=	a long life
stress	=	hypertension

p. 83

1. Topic: . . . aspects of a lifestyle that can lead to good health.
2. Ideas: A positive mental attitude, regular exercise, and a well-balanced diet. Three.
3. What contributes to good health?
4. Answers will vary.

p. 85

Exercise 1

1. lacks support.
2. lacks support.
3. the supporting ideas don't have the same level of generality.

CHAPTER five

p. 99 Using Quotations. Possible answers:

1. The source is Adam Dakin, Director of Marketing at Cardiovascular Imaging Systems.
2. Yes.
3. The quote helps explain the role of micromachines in medicine.

pp. 105–106 Essay Development Questions

1. The advantages of computers in education; paragraphs devoted to benefits.
2. Supporting ideas: benefits for teachers and students. Yes.
3. Transitions include repetition of key ideas (paragraphs 1 to 2), an additional consideration ("Not only . . . but also") (paragraphs 2 to 3), and a consolidation at the end.
4. There are both concrete and relevant details.
5. Yes.

pp. 106–107

Exercise 3
The thesis statement should be something such as "Although technology has improved our lives in many ways, it has also introduced some conditions that make our lives more difficult."

CHAPTER six

pp. 112–113 Getting Started

1. Answers are categorized facts from the text.
2. Solectron Corp.
3. Solectron Corp.
4. Answers will vary/are derived from student experience/opinion.

p. 114 Prereading Questions

1. Answers will vary.
2. Silicon Valley is in northern California. It's known for having a high concentration of high tech/computer companies. Some Silicon Valley companies are Apple Computer (personal computers) and Hewlett-Packard (computers, printers, etc.)
3. A new company, one that is just starting operations.
4. Money coming into a company; income.

p. 117 Thinking Critically. Answers will vary. Possible answers:

- It may have been more difficult for Alker because she's a woman.
- It may have been easier for Kahn because he's a man and from a European country/culture, where there are/may be more similarities in business practices.

pp. 122–123

Exercise 2 (key concepts)
Paragraph **A:** the capital of other nations to build.
Paragraph **B:** . . . Shaklee; successful; the managers understand the importance of giving.

p. 124

Exercise 6
Paragraph **A:** Eliminate repetition of *relationships* in all but the first and last sentences. Some possible substitutes are *friends in business, friendships,* or *get along well with people* instead of *have good relationships.*
Paragraph **B:** Some paraphrases for stubborn and inflexible: *independent, consistent, uncompromising.*

CHAPTER seven

pp. 134–135 Postreading Questions

1. The chart should look like this:

I. Summer Games
   A. Track and field events
   B. Gymnasium competition
   C. Water sports
   D. Team events
   E. Riding competition

I. Winter Games
   A. Skiing
      1. Jumping
      2. Cross country
      3. Downhill
      4. Slalom
   B. Ice skating
      1. Speed
      2. Figure
   C. Team sports
      1. Ice hockey
      2. Bobsledding

p. 136 Thinking Critically

Olympics >; downhill skiing =; winter events =; winter events >; weight lifting <; cycling <; team events >; ice skating =.

p. 145

Exercise 1: Suggestion for developing paragraph **A:**

My favorite vacation was the one I took several years ago. I met a couple of friends in central California during spring break, and we camped on the coast. The weather was warm and sunny, and we hiked, explored tidepools, and spent time as tourists too. We saw lots of wildlife, such as bobcats, raccoons, and gray foxes, and visited Hearst Castle and the old fishing village of Cambria. We met some nice people camping next to us. They were a retired couple traveling from Portland, Oregon, to Los Angeles to see their first grandchild. I'll never forget that vacation because my friends and I had time to take a break from school and catch up on each other's news. I hope we can meet again next year.

Exercise 2: Suggestion for developing paragraph **A:**

Watching TV has both advantages and disadvantages. One advantage is that it provides entertainment. I love to spend my Friday evenings relaxing in front of an old movie or a couple of funny situation comedies. Another advantage of watching TV is that it may also be informative or educational. I have learned a lot about wild animals, popular movie stars, and history from documentaries. I also keep up on current affairs by watching the news. On the other hand, there are some disadvantages to watching TV. First of all, it is a passive activity. We often choose to sit and eat in front of the TV instead of participating in more active (and healthy) activities like taking a walk, gardening, or bike riding. It may also take us away from other things we should be doing, such as reading or writing or talking with friends and family members. Therefore, there are both positive and negative aspects of watching TV.

CHAPTER eight

p. 155 Thinking Critically. Answers will vary. Two ways to explain the metaphor:

1. The past is an important part of the present.
2. A person's origins play a large role in who they are today.

p. 163

Exercise 2

Paragraph **A** follows the XYXY pattern.
Paragraph **B** follows the XXXXYYYY pattern.

CHAPTER nine

pp. 181–182

Exercise on city planners

1. The topic is using space in city planning. It is general.
2. The topic of sentence 4 is the Arch of Triumph as an example of the radiating star. It is specific.
3. Each sentence is more specific than the one that comes before it. Sentence 3 is more specific than sentence 2.
4. The pattern might look like this:

   Sentence 1
      Sentence 2
         Sentence 3 or
            Sentence 4

pp. 182–183

Exercise on use of space in different cultures

1. The topic is space in city planning; two parts; same.
2. The topic is the radiating star; one of the major systems; more specific.
3. The topic is the "grid" (another example of a system), more specific than sentence 1.
4. Sentence 3 is the same level of generality as sentence 2. Sentence 4: more specific. Sentence 5: more specific. Sentence 7: more specific than sentence 6. Sentence 8: more specific.
5. The pattern might look like this:

   Sentence 1
      Sentence 2
         Sentence 3
            Sentence 4
               Sentence 5 or
   Sentence 6
      Sentence 7
         Sentence 8

CHAPTER ten

p. 204 Exposing Weaknesses in Opposing Arguments

1. The *if* condition clause can come either at the beginning or the end of a sentence.
2. When the condition clause comes at the beginning of a sentence, it must be followed by a comma.
3. The condition clauses present the opposite point of view, the counterargument.
4. The example clauses are all in the present tense (even when referring to a point in the future, as in sentence 3).

pp. 208–209 Summarizing

1. The original article is eleven paragraphs long; the summary is one paragraph long.
2. The first sentence presents the topic of the paragraph, and it contains the main idea of Bennett's article.
3. The same main ideas are discussed in both the original article and the summary.
4. The order is the same.
5. Details have been eliminated.
6. Bennett's ideas are expressed in the summary; this is stated in the first paragraph ("According to William J. Bennett . . ."); the summary-writer's opinions do not appear in the summary.
7. "Bennett claims . . ."; "Bennett does not agree . . ."; "Bennett concludes . . .," etc.
8. Yes; "*greater parental involvement*" (paraphrase); "*justice system*" (copy).

CHAPTER eleven

pp. 218–219 Getting Started

1. Tahiti
2. Taos, New Mexico
3. Los Angeles, California
4. Alaska
5. Peru
6. Mekong River, Thailand

p. 226 Gathering Information. Here are some answers to get you started:

1. The Hunzukuts (see Chapter Four).
3. *Manifest Destiny* refers to westward expansion in U.S. history. Americans became accustomed to having an unexplored "frontier" to move to and felt that their destiny was to expand to the Pacific.

CHAPTER twelve

p. 244 Thinking Critically. Answers will vary. Possible examples of dated language:

"privileged by atrocious laws"; "perchance"; "smirchless."